WALKING WITH
JESUS
on the Natchez Trace

WALKING WITH
JESUS
on the Natchez Trace

A Common Man's Encounter
With God

REDEMPTION
PRESS

Troy A. Waugh

© 2020 by Troy A. Waugh. All rights reserved.

Published by Redemption Press, PO Box 427, Enumclaw, WA 98022.

Toll-Free (844) 2REDEEM (273-3336)

Redemption Press is honored to present this title in partnership with the author. The views expressed or implied in this work are those of the author. Redemption Press provides our imprint seal representing design excellence, creative content, and high-quality production.

No part of this publication may be reproduced, stored in a retrieval system, or transmitted in any way by any means—electronic, mechanical, photocopy, recording, or otherwise—without the prior permission of the copyright holder, except as provided by USA copyright law.

The author has tried to recreate events, locales, and conversations from his memories of them. In order to maintain their anonymity, in some instances he has changed the names of individuals and may have changed some identifying characteristics and details, such as physical properties, occupations, and places of residence.

Unless otherwise indicated, Scripture quotations marked NIV are taken from the Holy Bible, New International Version®, NIV® Copyright ©1973, 1978, 1984, 2011 by Biblica, Inc.® Used by permission. All rights reserved worldwide.

Scripture quotations marked ESV are taken from the ESV® Bible (The Holy Bible, English Standard Version®), copyright © 2001 by Crossway, a publishing ministry of Good News Publishers. Used by permission. All rights reserved.

Scripture quotations marked MSG are taken from THE MESSAGE, copyright © 1993, 2002, 2018 by Eugene H. Peterson. Used by permission of NavPress. All rights reserved. Represented by Tyndale House Publishers, Inc.

ISBN: 978-1-64645-008-4 (Paperback)
       978-1-64645-009-1 (ePub)
       978-1-64645-010-7 (Mobi)

Library of Congress Catalog Card Number: 2020900741

Dedication

To Sheryl Waugh, my wife, best friend, and partner on our walk with Jesus

To Ken Powers, a mentor and friend and an example of how the Lord can change our lives in dramatic ways

Dedication

Introduction

PLEASE JOIN ME ON A spiritual journey along the Natchez Trace Parkway from Natchez, Mississippi, to Nashville, Tennessee. This book relates a journey of spiritual renewal and rediscovery. While it does describe what I encountered on this historic parkway, this is not a hiking or nature book. It is about my walk with Jesus and how He has loved me even during the times I may have strayed from Him.

In 2014 I experienced a deepening of my relationship with Jesus like no other. This book is about that cleansing and invigorating experience. My prayer is that you, too, will feel God's love for you and you will recommit yourself to loving Jesus.

These thirty-one chapters are based upon notes from the daily journal I kept throughout the hike. Each of the days is unique, and each day God revealed Himself to me in a different way.

I trust your spirit will be renewed as I share some of my experiences of angels' visits, hearing the audible voice of God, the move of the Holy Spirit, a shocking suicide, the miracle of a change in the climate, and the renewed life that comes from turning your life over to God.

Troy Waugh

Contents

Introduction vii

Chapter 1: A New Beginning 11
Chapter 2: Getting Ahead of God 19
Chapter 3: Workaholics Can Be Saved 27
Chapter 4: Becoming a Christ Follower 35
Chapter 5: Living the Christian Life 41
Chapter 6: Relationships Matter 47
Chapter 7: The Church and Me 53
Chapter 8: What Is Love? 61
Chapter 9: The Power of the Holy Spirit 71
Chapter 10: Faith Is the Foundation 77
Chapter 11: Disciplines of a Disciple 85
Chapter 12: Facing Trials 93
Chapter 13: Life Is Hard 101
Chapter 14: Healing Is a Journey 111
Chapter 15: Dealing with Rejection 117
Chapter 16: The Power of God 123

Chapter 17: Hearing the Voice of God 131
Chapter 18: Listening Prayer 137
Chapter 19: God's Heart for Work 143
Chapter 20: Forming New Habits 149
Chapter 21: Goals, Plans, and Prayer 157
Chapter 22: God and Money 163
Chapter 23: A New Career 169
Chapter 24: Idols Take the Stage 175
Chapter 25: Choices Make a Life 179
Chapter 26: Joy—Heaven on Earth 185
Chapter 27: Discipleship and Leadership 193
Chapter 28: Selective Sins 201
Chapter 29: Correction and Judgment 207
Chapter 30: Who Is Jesus? 215
Chapter 31: God and Government 221

Afterword: Reflections on the Journey 229
Acknowledgments 231

Chapter 1

A New Beginning

Light yourself on fire with passion and people will come from miles to watch you burn.
—John Wesley

June 30, 2014

On Monday, May 5, 2014, as I was walking in the country, God spoke to me in an audible voice, "I want you to walk the Natchez Trace." Only one other time in my life had God spoken to me in an audible voice. God's direction for my life has almost always taken the form of an internal urging, a strong sense of what I am to do and a continual urging over a period of time. On this day, His voice spoke to me in such a manner that I heard it through my ears. It wasn't a thunderous voice. It wasn't a deep voice. It wasn't a southern voice. It wasn't in King James English. It was a masculine voice that spoke clearly to me and said, "I want you to walk the Natchez Trace."

This historic Natchez Trace Parkway runs from Natchez, Mississippi, to Nashville, Tennessee, through some of the most pristine land in the southern United States. I live in Leiper's Fork, Tennessee, so I was generally familiar with the trace but had driven only the portion between my home to Nashville, a distance of about twenty miles. I'd heard how beautiful the entire trace is. However, the speed limit is fifty miles an hour, and the ticket for violating the limit is a federal violation, so I'd always taken the interstate system.

I thought about how that has been a metaphor for my life: I was often in too much of a hurry to enjoy the beauty in life.

During the first few days of hearing my orders, God shared with me that I should deepen my relationship with others. Just walking for no particular reason would strike many people as odd. So God gave me an objective: to raise awareness and money for Community Care Fellowship (CCF), a homeless ministry in East Nashville I have supported for many years.

My original plan was to complete the 444 miles in thirty-one calendar days, walking twenty-seven of them and finishing on my seventieth birthday, August 1. Instead, my walk took thirty-five days, finishing up on August 4.

In this age of extreme marathons, Ironman competitions, and ninja warriors, there is really nothing amazing about an almost seventy-year-old man walking 444 miles in thirty-five days. But in recent years, my idea of a good workout had been to fill the bathtub with water, pull the plug, and fight the current as the water drained (thanks, Zig Ziglar for the idea).

God empowered me to accomplish a physical feat far beyond my personal power. He gave me the challenge and carried me through a journey that averaged a half-marathon daily. Along the way, He provided me insights into our relationship that will propel me through my remaining years.

To seriously connect to God, we must blot out the noise of our daily lives. Some people visit a monastery; some attend a retreat; others have their daily quiet time with the Lord. The method God chose for me in 2014 was to get away from my home, my friends, and family and spend time walking with Jesus on the Natchez Trace.

At 5:00 p.m. on June 30, 2014, day one of my journey began. My wife, Sheryl, dropped me off at the entrance to the Natchez Trace at mile marker zero and took a few photos. My feet were prepared, my shoes and socks were clean and dry, and my soul was ready to be filled.

Like a horse heading for the barn, I was in a hurry to get started, to renew, and to discover.

That morning I had awakened about an hour before the alarm sounded. During that hour I prayed, drank some coffee, and ate. During my prayer time, the Lord revealed a subject for my day's reflections.

The temperature was nearly ninety degrees, a typical southern Mississippi summer day. I felt full of excitement and energy. Within a few minutes, I was walking at about 3.5 miles an hour, a pace I could maintain for about two hours. Soon the sweat began pouring, and the mosquitoes started buzzing around me.

The paved roadway of the trace is wide, and there is a wide soft shoulder on either side. There are no billboards, no commercial signs, and no businesses located along the parkway, just pristine grasses, trees, ponds, and many animals. About thirty feet on either side of the parkway, magnolia, beech, long-leaf pine, red alder, and the invasive Chinese tallow trees were in full summer bloom.

Near mile marker one, I had an eerie sense that someone was following me. Sure enough, Sheryl was creeping along behind me in the Tahoe. She drove up beside me and flashed her movie-star smile. I loved that she wanted to keep an eye on me, but I said, "I'll meet you at the next rest stop."

Sheryl Jean Ferguson is a beautiful, courageous, and intelligent woman. Friendly and magnetic, she draws people to her naturally. I had been single for about five years and vowed I would never remarry, but after meeting Sheryl, my mind changed. I had never expected to meet such a giftedly practical, godly woman. When we met in 2009, she had lived the single life for nearly twenty-five years.

My wife was excited for my walk and wanted to share it with me. Over the next month, she walked many miles with me. That first day Sheryl went on ahead, and when I got to mile marker one, we held a small celebration.

Today's Reflections

This morning I prayed the Lord's Prayer from Matthew 6 and then sat quietly for about ten minutes or so in the presence of Jesus. The word *choices* crept into my consciousness. Perhaps the Holy Spirit was directing me to reflect on choices I've made and their impact on my past life.

As I walked those first miles, I thought back to when God had prompted the journey.

I had sold my business, the Rainmaker Companies, at the end of 2013 and didn't know what to do with my time. Rainmaker was a company I had started in 1991 after a previous urging from God. It had grown to become the largest of its kind in the world and was the capstone of my career, a gift from God. It was my baby and perhaps my idol.

From 1992 through 2013, I consulted and trained thousands of CPAs in thirty-five countries, traveled between one hundred and two hundred nights per year, wrote several books, and spoke at numerous conferences. I was recognized as a leader in the accounting profession. For ten consecutive years, I was recognized as being among the top one hundred most influential in the accounting industry.

For twenty-two years I had been in demand, and my life had been go-go-go. But now the calls had stopped coming, and my team had moved on without me.

I felt lost. In early May 2014, about four months after selling my business, my life seemed to have no purpose, no goal, and no reason. I felt like I'd been put out to pasture. For over four months I felt depressed, old, and useless. The team of professionals I had recruited, trained, loved, and worked alongside no longer needed my input. I felt rejected, abandoned, and depressed. The depression and gloom overwhelmed me like a dark cloud enveloping my soul. I felt as if I couldn't breathe and might drown at any moment. These gloomy feelings seemed to worsen by the day. I felt like lying down and giving up. At the time, my physical energy was weak, and I had no enthusiasm for my future.

But thanks be to God, He gave me a new life. He gave me a purpose. He gave me the will to fight back through this journey.

That's where I was when God spoke to me. May 5, 2014. I was rounding a curve in the road on a morning walk by Tim's Ford Lake. I clearly heard out loud, "I want you to walk the Natchez Trace."

"What's the Natchez Trace?" I was aware of the trace that goes from my home to Nashville, and that is what I thought He meant at first.

God said, "The parkway that runs from Natchez, Mississippi, to Nashville."

"Why the Natchez Trace?"

From this point on, I did not hear His audible voice, just the urging of the Holy Spirit, who said, *Do what I ask you to do, and you'll learn why.*

"Okay, Lord," I said, "when should I do this?"

The Holy Spirit said, *Start on July 1 and complete your walk on August 1, your seventieth birthday.*

I didn't do anything about it right away, but as each day progressed, the Holy Spirit became more intense in His direction. Within a week, I began to research the Natchez Trace and learned that it was indeed a federal parkway from Natchez to Nashville.

After about ten days, I shared with Sheryl the direction I was receiving.

"Are you crazy?" She knew I had never done anything like this before. Her questions began pouring out. "Why is God giving you this thing to do?"

"I'm not sure, but I'll find out."

"Why July?"

July was predicted to be the hottest, most humid month of the year in southern Mississippi and the mosquitoes would be swarming.

"Can't you wait until October? The weather will be nicer, and you'll have more time to train."

Sheryl was worried about me. "You are not in any physical shape to do this. How will you get ready?" She knew years of sitting at a desk, traveling by plane, train, and automobile, and engaging in meetings, had robbed my body of fitness.

I had no answer except, "The Holy Spirit told me to."

Telling someone God has instructed you to do something normally shuts down the conversation. They may reply, "Well, if God told you to do it, then I guess you'd better."

Or the bold ones will say, "Who are you for God to talk to?"

Most people would think, *This dude is nuts and he's blaming it on God.*

Sheryl was greatly skeptical, so she kept asking questions and giving her opinion. She may have been thinking of the adage: "When we talk to God, it's prayer, but when He talks to us, it is schizophrenia." But she was kind and didn't make me an appointment with the psychiatrist right away.

15

Troy Waugh

Today's Reflections

Every choice we make is a new beginning, a fresh first day. Why the choice to walk 444 miles in a month? Why a radical choice that was so out of character for me? This walk was a door to a new beginning for me, to a more exciting future, to a deeper relationship with my God and my family.

New beginnings are not easy. To make significant changes, I knew I had to commit to some hard work. How many times had I dieted to lose ten pounds only to gain twelve back? How many times had I started a workout routine, paid for the gym membership, and dropped out? How many times had I committed to love Jesus more, pray more, and study more before backsliding within a week?

Psychologists tell us we have certain characteristics with which we are born and certain traits we learn. These traits become habits or addictions or coping mechanisms that may be carried throughout our lives. These mechanisms certainly helped us cope when we were young but often sabotage us as we mature.

The apostle Paul said in Romans 7:15, "I do not understand what I do. For what I want to do I do not do, but what I hate I do." Paul may have been referring to the habits he learned in his youth but needed to change as he matured. In some ways, I often feel the unresolved trauma of my first years has kept me six years old.

I wrote a poem that expresses how I felt.

Will I Be Heard?

In the depths of my soul
There is a person I want to know.
He has a new life,
The old one boxed up and sealed.
He has left behind a life he tried to love,
To enter a life of aloneness,
A life of solitude,
A life plumbing the deep and the dark
Of the temple of the silent heart.

A New Beginning

This man has no one to visit,
Nowhere to go,
No crises to solve,
No masquerade ball.

The afternoon of the first day of my walk, a change came over me, the same change that always occurs whenever I move from one stage of life to another. I felt my pulse quickening as if with the excitement of a new love, the sharpening of my senses, and the sudden awareness of my body and soul taking on a new direction.

After I had walked nine miles on this first day, Sheryl and I were ready for dinner and rest. Driving back to the motel after dinner, I noticed one of the tires had a nail in it. So before going to bed, I stayed up until 10:00 p.m. to meet AAA for the tire change. Once in bed, I tossed and turned until 4:00 a.m. when it was time to get on with the next day.

Only 435 miles to go! While I had confidence I would reach this goal, I knew there are many goals in life I can never reach. But I was confident that in reaching out for important things, I could be renewed and discover joy. Reaching for perfection, for the stars, for my true soul would keep me busy praying and extending.

I determined this would be a walking sabbatical, a time of reflection on lessons I've learned, people I've known, and experiences in life, in business, and in the power of God. At the center of my soul is a man I wanted to get to know. It would be a real tragedy to arrive at the end of my life and not know myself or for my family and friends not to know the real me.

I was choosing a life that is directional. Today I attained mile marker 9. Tomorrow it would be on to the end of the trace, day by day, step by step, just as I would walk on with Jesus from here to eternal life.

Chapter 2

Getting Ahead of God

Nine-tenths of the difficulties are overcome when our hearts are ready to do the Lord's will, whatever it may be. When one is truly in this state, it is usually but a little way to the knowledge of what His will is.
—George Muller

July 1, 2014

TODAY WAS A DAY I had eagerly anticipated. Although my sleep was fitful, pure excitement propelled me from the bed before the alarm sounded.

As I sipped my morning coffee, the Holy Spirit reminded me that today was to be my start day, not yesterday. Praying for several minutes gave me the assurance that the Lord's grace was with me as I prepared for today's walk. Thank you, Father.

Several times in the Old Testament, God ended people's lives for doing something different than instructed. I recalled the story of Uzzah and the ark of the covenant (2 Sam. 6:1–7). Was that my lesson for the day? Don't get ahead of God. Don't do things Troy's way, do things God's way. I felt God had helped me plot the course of my walk as I began to train for the journey. Was He going to strike me down today? Had I already failed?

Sheryl drove me to the nine-mile marker to begin the morning's walk. At 6:10 a.m., the Mississippi air was still comfortable as the morning sun was starting to break on the horizon. The kaleidoscope of colors, the slivers of early daylight slicing through the clouds, and the vanishing shadows were all breathtaking.

The walk that began with excitement was replaced with a few moments of despair and a feeling that I had returned to my old home of shame. Then I recalled Romans 8:1, "There is no condemnation for those who are in Christ Jesus." Rather than starting my trek feeling shame, I chose to dwell on the truth. My confidence was restored as God reminded me of His grace, love, and forgiveness.

At about 6:15 a.m. Russ Corley sent me a message, "What's your plan for the day?"

"Morning, Russ," I texted. "I got a little ahead with nine miles last night, and I plan for twelve more this morning."

"You can do it," Russ shot back.

Russ Corley had become my daily encouragement coach. Leader of Encouragement Ministries, he deals with people encountering hard times, death, illness, loss, divorce, or pain. An ordained minister, Russ was fired from his church about twenty-five years ago for washing the feet of his elders. Shaken but not disillusioned, he formed his ministry and has walked daily with the Lord, visiting the sick and dying and being obedient to his calling all these years.

Today's Reflections

The first few miles went quickly as I talked to God and listened for today's lessons. I knew I needed to understand myself better so I could serve God and others. Today God seemed to be directing me to look back over major events in my life.

I was born August 1, 1944, immediately after my dad, William Troy Waugh, was assigned to the war zone in Germany under General George Patton. Dad helped liberate Nazi concentration camps and set up the post-war military government. Dad did not volunteer much about the death and destruction he experienced though he brought home photos reflecting the horrors of the camps and the mass graves. He just did what millions of other surviving service members did—he went about working hard to raise and support a family.

When my father returned from the war zone, my mother, my

grandfather, and I met him at the train. Dad was excited to come home after the horrors of war. He'd tell the story about how the waiting crowd gave a collective gasp as each soldier or sailor stepped off the train. Years later, Dad shared how he was emotionally crushed when he got off the train in Chattanooga and I clung to my grandfather's neck. I had lived most of the first year of my life in my grandfather's home, so it was understandable I wouldn't immediately reach out for my real dad, but he felt deeply hurt.

My sister, Alice Carol, whom I adored, was born in 1947. One day my parents couldn't locate me. After searching the house and yard, they finally found a dirty big brother in Alice's cradle with my arm wrapped around her. That is how it has been with Alice; I was her big brother who protected her.

Alice's nature was completely opposite to mine in many ways. She was a great student with an agreeable disposition. We do share the qualities of hard work, determination, and creativeness—and workaholism. She was a straight-A student in school, played basketball, and developed a flair for art. Alice majored in art at Carson Newman College, taught high school art, and eventually had her own art gallery.

Mischief and Punishment

I was a curious and adventuresome kid who was in some type of mischief at least weekly. If I got into trouble in school, my parents would punish me doubly hard when I got home. My mother initiated most of the corporal punishment with slaps, switches, and belts. Every so often my dad would administer the whipping. I recall being punished at times with "just because," the reason spit at me.

That kept our house very tense and elevated my level of anxiety to a high degree. During one particularly harsh whipping, I escaped into the bathroom, locked the door, and climbed out the window to avoid the punishment. That was the first time I ventured away from home on my own. I walked nearly ten miles to the store where my father worked to appeal to his sense of fairness. It didn't do any good; he took me home and completed the punishment.

Whippings, beatings, and slaps were normal and regular. My sister described them as being in a terrorist camp. She was always fearful she would be punished like her older brother, so she kept a very low and compliant profile. My nature was defiant. Once after a severe whipping, I told my dad, "That didn't hurt." So he proceeded to show me what hurt felt like, and hurt me he did.

When roads were installed in a new subdivision under development behind our house, they became great bike-riding surfaces. The cul-de-sacs were also good places for guys to bring their girlfriends. To get me to leave, guys would roll down their fogged-up windows and give me a quarter. I learned to listen for cars so I could ride my bike up and collect the toll.

While we lived in Chattanooga, I picked pecans. We would keep some of them, but I would go door to door and sell small bags of pecans to our neighbors. I also learned to make pot holders with a small square loom and a stretchy fabric that sold for a dime each.

These early years formed the patterns for a lifetime and the beginnings of my becoming an entrepreneur.

Ms. Hendrix was my fourth-grade teacher, a very dedicated lady whom I enjoyed very much. One day one of the girls in the class and I got into a silly game of chase. Ms. Hendrix held me responsible. She had me bend over her desk in front of the class to paddle me with a wooden paddle. The first time she whacked my butt, I whirled around, grabbed the paddle from her, and threw it out the window. She called the vice-principal to take over. He took me into the hallway, had me bend over a water fountain, and commenced to finish the paddling job. I whirled around on him, but he was stronger. The more I tried to resist, the tighter he held me with his left hand. Then he lost his temper and began whipping me with all his might, blow after blow after blow. He was sweating and angry, and I was hurting badly.

He sent me back to my classroom to my desk, where it was very painful to sit. About an hour later, he called me out of class again.

What else have I done?

"Listen, if you don't tell your parents about that whipping, I won't say any more about it."

I didn't want to report it to my parents because any time there was trouble at school, it was much worse at home. So I kept quiet.

When my mother noticed the black and blue bruises on my butt and thighs, she quizzed me about what happened. I was shaking in fear of getting another beating. That was the only time ever my parents didn't punish me further. My parents visited the principal and vice-principal the next day, and I never heard any more about it.

By ten years of age, I had grown a hard outer shell, a coping strategy I used effectively as a child and overused as an adult. When I entered sixth grade, I was the youngest and smallest in my class, so I became a target for the bullies. Being the defiant, you-can't-hurt-me type, I fought back any way I could. I learned if I hit first when I sensed trouble, I could protect myself from the big boys. Most of them would back off.

Once I was agitating a bigger boy who had threatened me. I hit him with my fist, and he backed off for the moment. About a half hour later, he hit me in the mouth with a football helmet and knocked my teeth through my lips. I bled profusely and had to have stiches.

Every person is created and nurtured into a mosaic of personality patterns, tendencies, habits, and sometimes addictions. Most of these patterns are formed in the early childhood. As I have looked back on my youth with the help of counseling, I have uncovered parts of myself of which I hadn't been aware.

Who Am I?

When I was eight years old, my parents led me to a belief in Jesus Christ as my personal Savior. Being a Christian does not mean I am a perfect person; it means my sins have been forgiven and I have eternal life. But rather than obtaining my sense of worth as an adopted child of God, I have assessed my value from my deeds.

Anger is one of my "protector parts" that ignites when things don't go my way.

Perseverance became an internal drive to succeed that helped me achieve some level of success in life. I am very goal oriented, so having and achieving goals motivates me.

To relieve the guilt from failures, I tended to cover up my missteps with lightheartedness and my sense of humor.

The attraction to money has often taken precedence over God, my family, my health, my mind, my body, and my neighbors.

I did not experience a loving family when I was young and have only learned to appreciate its value as I have matured.

I am a quick starter. My tendency is to ready, fire, aim. I can often begin acting with little direction or information, often foolishly.

Learning to lie to avoid punishment as a child, I carried this coping strategy into adulthood unnecessarily.

Many of these traits make me aggressive, so I often run over people.

On the other hand, my father taught me to be generous, and I do give away time and resources regularly.

My morning walk was scheduled for about four hours. It felt amazing as I walked past each mile marker. The first mile was a huge celebration. Then as the mile markers ticked by, it was more of an attaboy with a little fist pump. With fourteen new miles under my belt, I finished around 10:35 a.m., ahead of schedule. After recovering from the restless night and the excitement of beginning my walk, it was time for some chocolate milk and rest.

Natchez Mounds

On my walk today I discovered two beautiful historic sites. At mile marker 10 (MM 10) is the Emerald Mound, an enormous Indian burial ground that was used from 1250 to 1600. The size and scope of this mound is incredible at 770 feet by 385 feet wide and 35 feet high.

At MM 15 stands the Mount Locust Inn, one of two original structures still on the trace from early in the nineteenth century, reflecting the primitive lodging available along the trace for Ohio Valley farmers returning home from market.

During the afternoon, Sheryl and I explored some of the beautiful old mansions of Natchez. Shaped by African, French, British, and Spanish settlers, Natchez is a quaint southern town with a rich culture. The area's first inhabitants were the ancestors of the Natchez Indians. In about 1716, French explorers first came to the area and made peace with the tribe. The Natchez tribe inhabited the area from the AD 8 through the French colonial period.

At Grand Village of the Natchez Indians are the surviving Natchez mounds, which were consecrated holy ground for the Indians around

AD 1200. The village center was the hub of life from 1682 to 1729. There are several reconstructed buildings and burial mounds.

When the Natchez warred with the French, they were wiped out. Shortly after French settlers arrived, they brought slaves from West Africa to what would become the state of Mississippi.

I imagined a farmer from Ohio or Kentucky floating on a wooden flatboat down the Ohio River to the mighty Mississippi River with his year's harvest. Farmers would float the rivers or streams from their homes to the Mississippi, then on to New Orleans or Natchez to sell their crops. After selling their crops, the farmers would sell the wood from their boats. Without power, they could not return upstream. With the money from their endeavors, they began the walk back to their homes along the path I was now following. They walked day after day without the seven weeks of training I'd had, without the good bed of the Hampton Inn, without the Saucony walking shoes, without a loving wife driving alongside for assistance. Many of them were robbed or killed for their money on the dangerous trip home.

As I walked a couple of hours into the evening, temperatures had risen to ninety-five degrees Fahrenheit, and the heat and humidity felt overwhelming. Within a few minutes the sweat began pouring down my back like the mighty Mississippi River itself. The mosquitoes and gnats swarmed, and I was swatting wildly like a derelict walking the alleys of downtown Nashville.

While Sheryl had been a reluctant partner in my venture, she began to embrace the time she had to be alone with God and to journal her thoughts. Tonight over dinner she shared some of her heart with me. She said God had been speaking to her, especially while she prayed at a pull-off beside the trace.

Chapter 3

Workaholics Can Be Saved

Developing a good work ethic is key. Apply yourself at whatever you do, whether you're a janitor or taking your first summer job, because that work ethic will be reflected in everything you do in life.
—Tyler Perry

July 2, 2014

UNLIKE YESTERDAY, THE 4:00 A.M. buzzer jarred me awake with the urgency of a drill sergeant. As I reluctantly dressed and grabbed my coffee, my prayers were labored and distracted. *Will I hear from the Lord today?*

I prayed, "Oh, Lord I am tired, I am weak, and I am weary, and it is just day three." I jotted a note:

> **Anticipation**
>
> Ever roiled through
> One of those nights?
> Dreading,
> Yearning,
> Questioning,
> Anticipating, and
> Knowing you will step into your possibilities today.

During the drive to the starting point, the clouds moved in, and the rain gushed like a waterfall. I praised God for the gift of the rain as an excuse to stop walking and rest. Back in bed, my head hit the pillow, and I slept soundly for three more hours. Oh man, that felt good.

After a light lunch, Sheryl dropped me back off at the marker. For the first twenty minutes, I laid my heart before the Lord. Had the storm not canceled my plans that morning, I would have pushed on toward the goal. I had lost touch with my need for ample rest. Without it, our bodies and minds lose the ability to function well.

As a workaholic, I have spent much of my life in the dizzying fog created from overwork. God is showing me why I've made poor decisions when I've operated at near burnout.

A combination of the midday heat of ninety-eight degrees, the humidity from the morning rain, and my listless energy required me to call it after an hour. Even though I was rested, I walked only three miles in an hour before I called it quits, a much slower pace than usual. I was so glad Sheryl had waited for me at a rest stop, but I was sad I had to cut the day's walk short.

Sheryl said, "I know you are really bummed out about it, but I feel it was God's way of having you get the rest you need."

During the afternoon, we drove to Port Gibson, Mississippi, just off the parkway between Vicksburg and Natchez. There we checked into the Isabella Bed and Breakfast Inn. The Isabella is a quaint historic home featuring 1880 Queen Anne architecture. It's listed on the National Register as the Person Home. The Isabella is a great stop for history buffs and offers plenty of southern hospitality. Sheryl loved the Singer treadle sewing machines made into nightstands as that is the machine on which she learned to sew.

We enjoyed strolling around the streets of Port Gibson, viewing the beautiful homes and churches. Chartered as a town in 1803, Port Gibson is Mississippi's third-oldest European-American settlement. It was developed beginning in 1729 by French colonists, at that time within French-claimed territory known as La Louisiana.

Port Gibson was the site of several clashes during the American

Civil War and figured into Ulysses S. Grant's Vicksburg campaign. The Battle of Port Gibson occurred on May 1, 1863, and resulted in the deaths of over two hundred Union and Confederate soldiers. Many of the town's historic buildings survived the Civil War because Grant reportedly proclaimed the city to be "too beautiful to burn."

After a nap and one of Sheryl's invigorating leg rubs, she drove me to MM 31, and I launched into my evening walk with more energy and enthusiasm, ready to explore the things God had for me. Sheryl gave me a pep talk saying, "You can do it if you take it easy and don't push too hard." I had the sense that God was definitely with me every step. When I started to get too hot, I would often feel a cool breeze on my face.

Today's Reflections

As I walked, I thought about how perilous exhaustion is to the physical and spiritual body. While my exhaustion this day wasn't like some I had experienced, it prompted me to review those times in my life when I had exhausted myself and what God has to say to me about this.

It became clear that it was during times of exhaustion that I was most subject to sin, errors of judgment, mistakes, broken relationships, and failures.

We all look back over our lives and wonder what we might change if we could. I would dial back on the work and increase my love for my family and my Lord. While I do believe the grace of Jesus would have saved my soul had I died during this period, the many sins I committed would have generated a long list for which I needed to repent.

As I walked, I thought about my dad who died at age sixty-four. I wondered, *Why have I been blessed with this life? What does God have in store for me? What is He telling me? Will I learn the lessons?*

My Father

My father, William Troy Waugh, was a grocer and a workaholic who worked an average of ninety hours per week. He was a great dad, a kind, gentle, and outgoing person who led me to the Lord and modeled for me the human version of Jesus. I felt the pain of his early death.

He spent his annual two-week vacation training with the National

Guard, was a deacon in our church, and an active member in a service club. He was forced to retire about six months before he died of lung cancer.

My relationship with my dad centered on work. From age six, I stocked shelves with the labels turned forward, sacked groceries, and helped customers. From about twelve years of age, I worked after school and on weekends, up to thirty hours a week.

About once a year, my dad would take me fishing, always on Saturday night after the store closed. Three or four times, my dad obtained University of Tennessee football tickets. He made the ultimate sacrifice to take off a half day on a Saturday (the biggest shopping day of the week) to drive me to Knoxville for the ball game.

My father was born in 1913 in Yuma, Tennessee, and was a young teenager during the Great Depression, which gripped the United States from 1929 through 1938. Because of the economic hardship caused by the Great Depression, millions of people were traumatized for life. Many were fearful they might go hungry and not be able to feed themselves or their families.

Dad's parents were farmers, and their children were the workforce, and the farmwork was brutal. He learned to smoke at age eleven. In 1934, at age twenty-one, Dad left the farm to join the US Army. "No matter what," he'd say, "I wasn't going to go back to that farm."

Both my dad and my mom were products of the Great Depression. Both worked and worked and worked—mostly to avoid the possibility of poverty. This work ethic was ingrained into me and has been the source of my greatest successes and failures in life.

I had a little time to write this in my journal:

Your Gifts

> On the edge of the pit of your life,
> you expand the grace
> you have for your place.
> This place is yours.
> Your place is only yours—
> Never has your spot been lived.
> Never again will your star shine.
> It's yours, not his nor hers, not mine.

The pain and loss you've endured
is to build this grace
to love your whole life, the entire place.
This grief you feel for your loss
covers your guilt for not being there for him,
not knowing or understanding his place,
not saving him from his horror.

Because on the edge of his pit,
the pain was unbearable, excruciating.

So his place was brief,
yours may be long.
Dive into the west,
go into your pit,
the dark around the edges.
You may find a way to save your life
and bring your gifts to me.

Hard work became a habit, then an addiction. I became addicted to the adrenaline rush of the urgent. At age seventeen, I joined the US Navy and became a radioman on a submarine. At the time, submarines had a shortage of radiomen, and I had no problem working the twelve-hours-on-and-twelve-hours-off schedule. When we were in port, I would be on duty for twenty-four-hour shifts.

After active duty, I enrolled as a full-time student at the University of Tennessee, Knoxville. In addition, I continued in the Navy Reserve and worked full time at the Tennessee Valley Authority. By attending summer classes, I was able to complete my bachelor's degree in accounting within about three and a half years.

The workaholic pattern I learned while growing up seemed normal to me. I viewed with disdain those who didn't seem to be in as much of a hurry as slackers, or lazy.

A partner at PricewaterhouseCoopers (PwC) advised me, "If you will commit to work ten percent more, you will surpass others." Following his advice was easy. In addition, I began raising a family with my first wife, Carolyn Honeycutt, while studying for my MBA.

The PwC years were very helpful to my career. Accounting is the language of business, and I now had a ten-year foundation. During my PwC years, the partners asked me to lead the practice development committee, which was responsible for attracting new clients.

Although I was green as grass, our team enjoyed many successes and attracted many new clients. On one occasion, there was a large opportunity to approach a prospective client. I worked for a week on the proposal, practiced my sales presentation, and bought a brand-new suit to wear for the meeting with their board of directors. While making the presentation, the board members were smiling throughout the presentation and seemed very engaged with me. But as I got into the car for the drive back, I noticed the sales tag still hanging from the sleeve of my suit coat. No wonder they were amused.

At age thirty, I became CEO of a small publicly owned company, Advantage Companies, Inc. For the next eight years, my workaholic tendency moved into overdrive. From 1975 through 1983, I led the transformation of Advantage from a budget motel chain into a publishing company and prepared it for a major merger. During those years, I was involved in a dizzying array of property sales, refinances, business acquisitions, litigation, challenging financial audits, compliance with securities law, and employee turnover. Following my father's example, I worked ninety-hour weeks.

As a result of eight straight years of living in overdrive, I bankrupted my family physically, mentally, and spiritually. At the end of that experience, I was a wreck and took many years to heal. My addiction to work had become a soul-destroying preoccupation that numbed my feelings and caused me to lose both my personal and professional judgment and integrity. My lack of integrity eventually led to my family's breakup. With my judgment seriously impaired, I became emotionally crippled and addicted to power, greed, and control. While I played at other roles of life—father, husband, Christian brother—I became narrowly focused on accomplishment and success in business.

Looking back, I see I lacked the wisdom to balance my life and focus on my faith and family. Obsessed with my work performance, I was hooked on the adrenaline high of aiming for and successfully reaching one goal after another. I walked fast, talked fast, overscheduled, and always tried putting ten pounds of taters into a five-pound sack. I had given up exercise and regularly suffered from long bouts of insomnia.

Workaholics Can Be Saved

Needing to always be in control, I was proud of my independence, arrogance, and intensity. That intensity often provoked me to anger. However, I learned anger did not work well in business, and I worked on becoming sociable and witty when it served me well. I was impatient, impulsive, and demanding. As a result, I developed business contacts but very few real friends.

As I walked that day, I thanked God for adversity and the strength to leave an old pattern and develop a new one.

By the end of the day I had got to MM 40; I had covered another nine miles. I knew if I just kept on plodding I would eventually arrive in Nashville—one step and one mile at a time. I was well aware the quest for this goal must not take priority over what mattered most—communing with Jesus, loving my family and neighbors, and getting appropriate rest.

Chapter 4

Becoming a Christ Follower

*For God so loved the world that he gave his one and only Son,
that whoever believes in him shall not perish
but have eternal life.*
—John 3:16

July 3, 2014

THE ANXIOUS HIGHS AND LOWS of the last few days were beginning to calm. My body seemed to be adjusting. Eagerly arising before the alarm indicated my enthusiasm had recovered.

The old stairway of the historic antebellum home creaked as I made my way downstairs to the kitchen and the coffee pot. Bobbye Pinnix, the owner of the Isabella B and B, had prepared the pot so I just had to press the perk button. I sat down at the table and began my prayer time as the aroma of the coffee filled the kitchen.

Sheryl drove me to MM 40, and I began the walk right on time at 5:30 a.m. After a mile I came to the section of the original Natchez Trace called the Sunken Trace. I got a real sense of the eroded, time-worn path that made it easy for robbers to hide and hold up the farmers walking back home from market with their pockets full of money.

Troy Waugh

Today's Reflections

The Lord reminded me that morning how I became a Christ follower, so I began reflecting on my salvation: how it happened and what it meant. When I say salvation, I mean confessing and repenting of my sins, believing Jesus was fully God and fully human, that He was born of a virgin and died to atone for my sins, and accepting His lordship over my life.

For many years I believed simply accepting Him as my Savior punched my ticket to heaven. I now realize conversion is followed by a process of discipleship leading to sanctification. This is a continual process of accepting His perfect will and lordship of my life and becoming more like Christ.

My Faith Story

My parents were Christians, as were most of my relatives. Our family prayed at each meal. Both my father and mother studied the Bible, and my father taught Sunday school at our Southern Baptist church. We attended church as a family on Sunday mornings and evenings and Wednesday evenings as well other church-related activities.

My father had been raised in the Church of Christ denomination and my mother in the Baptist church. When they married, they settled on the Baptist church. That selection foretold the more dominant parent. Like the big argument in the Garden of Eden between Adam and Eve: Who would wear the "plants" in the family? My mom clearly wore the pants in our family, so to speak.

As a kid, I enjoyed experiencing the different Christian denominations with family and friends. My immediate family never taught a preeminence of one Christian denomination over the other. I relished sitting on the hill just outside a Pentecostal church near my uncle's home and hearing the joyful music and emotion emanating from their Sunday night services. The presence of the Holy Spirit through that music encouraged and inspired me.

At the Eastdale Baptist Church in Chattanooga, every Sunday morning and evening, Brother R. R. Denny held an altar call at the end of the service. After the singing, praying, and preaching, he gave people an opportunity to publicly accept Jesus. We would sing *all* the verses of "Just As I Am" until someone moved.

Becoming a Christ Follower

When I was eight years old, I walked down to the altar and accepted Christ on Easter Sunday, April 5, 1953. On any Sunday following a decision for Christ, there would be a baptism, with Brother Denny dressed in trout-fishing waders prepared to dunk those who were prepared.

On the following Sunday, I walked into the chilly water of the baptismal pool at the front of the church behind the pulpit. Brother Denny asked me again if I had accepted Christ as my personal Savior. Then he said, "In recognition of Troy Waugh answering the call of Jesus, I now baptize you in the name of the Father, the Son, and the Holy Spirit." He placed his left hand over my nose and mouth with a dry handkerchief and lowered me backward into the pool for a few seconds, then lifted me back up as the entire congregation applauded.

Brother Denny and other preachers said, "Accept Jesus and your life will be immediately changed." I assumed the very act of accepting Christ would remove all my bad deeds and habits. I assumed I would now obey my parents and teachers and would stop picking on my sister. I was totally unprepared for Satan's attacks on me as a new Christian.

Some years after I gave my life to Christ, I asked one of my navy shipmates about his faith.

"I'm a Christian," he said.

"How did you become one?"

I'll never forget how he responded. "I was born a Christian. I've gone to church all my life."

Those who belong to Christ know it's impossible to be born a Christian because we are born with a sin-infected nature, lost from God.

Over the years, I have come to understand more about what being a Christian is all about. What really happened on that Easter Sunday was this: On April 4, I was a lost sinner, and on April 5, I had become a saved sinner.

For decades, I completely missed the joy of deepening my relationship with the Lord; I failed to become a disciple of Jesus.

The apostle John says, "This is how God showed his love among us: He sent his one and only Son into the world that we might live through him" (1 John 4:9). The apostle Paul says, "If you declare with your mouth, 'Jesus is Lord,' and believe in your heart that God raised him from the dead, you will be saved" (Rom. 10:9). The moment we do so, the Holy Spirit makes us entirely new creatures in Christ (2 Cor. 5:17).

How can we tell if our salvation is real? Again, John says, "We know that we have come to know him if we obey his commands. Whoever says, 'I know him,' but does not do what he commands is a liar, and the truth is not in that person" (1 John 2:3–4).

A Christian, then, is a person who is born again by the Spirit of God, trusts in Jesus, and seeks to be obedient. Becoming a follower of Jesus Christ through the new birth is the most important step a person can make in this life and for the life hereafter.

No one is ever automatically a Christian by birth. To be a Christian, we each must make a conscious choice to turn from our sins—that's repentance—and by faith believe Jesus is the Son of God who loved us, paid the price for our sins on Calvary's cross, shed His blood and died, was buried, and was raised to life on the third day.

This morning I walked from 5:30 to 10:00 a.m. and covered twelve miles. I could feel the cumulative fatigue from walking fifty-two miles in four days. It seems my physical stamina has waned quite a bit, while my brain says, Push hard. My legs and knees ache, but some Advil, Aspercreme, and Sheryl's leg rubs all helped to calm the inflammation.

Spiritually, this morning was a good morning as I reflected on my faith and made a commitment to cultivate it more. While I had planned to walk again this evening, we decided to have dinner and rest after Sheryl reminded me of my reflections on rest yesterday.

We found a delightful little café, Rosie's, and enjoyed some Mississippi catfish. The server was very warm and entertaining as she cracked several jokes about the Ole Miss–UT football rivalry. There were only about twenty seats in Rosie's, and they all seemed to be taken by local folks. When they learned we were from Tennessee, many of them waved or stopped by our table and said hello.

The catfish was plump and fried crispy, just like we like it. The hush puppies and coleslaw were homemade and delicious. Best of all, Sheryl and I shared a piece of hot apple pie smothered with ice cream. Since Sheryl can't eat dairy, I cleaned up the vanilla bean ice cream all by myself. Sheryl slapped me playfully as I started to lick the plate.

Chapter 5

Living the Christian Life

The long painful history of the world is for people to be tempted to choose prestige and power over love, being in charge over being led, being served over serving others.
—Henri Nouwen

July 4, 2014

IN THOSE DREAMY MOMENTS BEFORE waking, I wondered what heaven was like. What will it be like to see Jesus every day? To walk beside Him? Will we eat food? Will we wear clothing? Will we go shopping, to church, to football games? Will we ride in cars or airplanes? Will my friends be surprised to see me?

On the fifth day of my walk, my physical energy felt strong as I stepped down the creaky old staircase to the coffeepot and my quiet time with the Lord. This morning my prayers led me to follow up on yesterday's reflections.

My friend Russ Corley texted, "What is your plan today?"

"I hope to make twelve to fifteen miles today by walking this morning as well as later in the afternoon," I texted.

Russ responded, "You can do it. I just prayed for you."

At 5:30 a.m., Sheryl drove me to MM 52 to begin. The morning air was crisp as the sun began to creep up the eastern horizon. All around me the Natchez Trace was alive with the sounds of nature—whitetail deer dashing through the woods and bluebirds singing in the trees. Today I felt quite normal and hoped to cover some good territory.

After the morning walk we returned to the Isabella for a shower, leg rub, and a little nap. Sheryl said, "I hate to leave this precious B and B." She had especially enjoyed the Victorian antiques, beautiful yards, and great southern hospitality of Port Gibson. The owners had left for Vicksburg and gave us the key to the house and told us to lock up when we left.

Today's Reflections

During my quiet time, the Lord encouraged me today to delve more deeply into my daily walk with Jesus.

For years my life did not really show any results of being a Christian. I failed most days to perform any of the Christian disciplines: prayer, reading God's Word from the Holy Bible, or worshiping in any manner. I was like the guy who had a nice set of clubs and called himself a golfer but only played at annual best-ball scrambles. Looking back, I lament I failed to experience the peace and joy of living the Christian life to the fullest.

While I had converted to Christianity, I did not grasp that I was now an adopted son of God. All the sin and shame that plagued me had been atoned for. All I needed to do was reach out to the power of Jesus to live the Christian life.

I completely missed the promise that God would transform me into the image of His Son. How could I possibly be transformed or sanctified? I intentionally sinned and allowed business successes and money to take the place of God. I intentionally lied. I intentionally committed adultery. In my mind, I couldn't possibly understand how God would still save me and want me to be His son.

Because I lived many years without walking conversationally with the Lord, my spiritual life was stunted. I've heard many pastors and teachers talk about an intimate walk with God. Sheryl models a conversational walk as she prays constantly in all situations. It was as if I had a spiritual handicap, but I was now on a walk to change that.

In 1967, while I was beginning my third year at UT, I married Carolyn Honeycutt. Carolyn had completed her degree at Carson Newman and held a social work position in Knoxville while I completed my degree. In February 1969, our twin girls were stillborn, as the umbilical cord from one had wrapped around the neck of the other. It was a devastating loss for us both.

Brad, our first son, was born August 5, 1970. We were delighted and overjoyed to have a healthy and beautiful boy. Early in Brad's life, he developed an affinity for music. One day when he was about seven, Scott Joplin's "The Entertainer" was playing on an audio tape in my car. Brad listened to it a few times. Once we got home, Brad sat down at the piano and picked out the song. Within an hour or so, we were amazed that he was playing it.

Brad was a top student and very engaged in the music program at school, where he played the saxophone and xylophone. He played baseball and junior pro football, but his love for music was paramount. He became the drum major for his high school band when he was a sophomore and in his senior year won first place in his division in the state for his performance. His band won many competitions and awards for excellence. When Brad graduated high school, he was awarded a music scholarship to the University of Miami, where he studied jazz piano.

Brad could argue with a signpost and win. After earning his master's at Rice University, he worked for a couple of years before attending law school at Stanford. He practiced intellectual property law with two large firms and is now in the IP litigation department at Intel Corporation.

Brad married Tara Maddala in 1998 and Brad and Tara have brought three beautiful grandchildren—Max, Miles, and Maya—into my world. Max excels as an athlete and chef and loves to prepare steaks or barbecue for PaPa when I visit. Max has a heart for other people and for Jesus. Miles is gifted in math and can solve a Rubik's cube in under one minute. Maya has grown into quite a leader, was selected president in her elementary school, and successfully led an effort to bring additional playground equipment to their school.

All three of Brad and Tara's children are gifted in music. For years they performed in a band they named The Waugh Zoo, now renamed The Waughs.

Troy Waugh

Beginning in about 1990, I began to slowly grow in my salvation over a period of years. My pastors and teachers challenged me to grow in my spiritual walk. As a result of living the life of a shallow Christian, I had outsourced the spiritual training of my children to the church. While I may have mouthed the right words, my actions belied those words and provided a poor example to my boys.

I've learned I am a Christian because God chose me from before the foundation of the world. I believe He chooses everyone. It is then up to us to choose Him back. I've learned the Bible is meant to be applied in our daily lives, here and now.

The most important thing I had to learn was to practice the spiritual disciplines of prayer, Bible study, and regular worship. I learned to look to Christ as my righteousness rather than to my own performance. The Lord opened my eyes to see the Bible teaches *inter*dependence. I am responsible to confess my sin, I am responsible to grow in the fruit of the Spirit, but I am dependent on the enabling power of the Holy Spirit.

Power comes from the Holy Spirit. I was proud of my individualism and always tried to do almost everything on my own. It had to be pounded into my thick skull that my power is small and His is infinite. I must depend upon God for the power to live the Christian life. In 2 Peter 1:3, Peter says, "His divine power has given us everything we need for life and godliness."

In the last few years, I've had an increased awareness of my absolute dependence on and my appreciation for the work of the Holy Spirit. While I continue to slip back from time to time, the Holy Spirit has helped me clean up much of my old self.

The salvation of the thief on the cross gives me hope for God's extravagant grace to cover my shortcomings. God has graciously saved me not through anything I have earned but because of his goodness. A friend once told me, "God's grace is like a cop not only forgiving my breaking the speed limit but giving me $500 as I drive away."

Sheryl's Notes

Troy is back on the trace as I type and wants to get in at least five more miles. Since I talked him into eating a little before his walk, he seems to be doing better. I think some of the fatigue this morning was not drinking enough and not eating enough food. He is a man, so should I say, a little stubborn! Jackson has a lot of traffic on the trace much like a regular highway, and I am not letting him out of my sight range. Someone might realize what a great man he is and want to pick him up!

We are truly learning as we travel this journey. We are having fun and thanking God for all he has blessed us with—especially family and friends. Every one of us has so much to be grateful for, so look around and see what sweet blessing God has given you today.

I did eleven miles on a slow incline today and wrapped up my morning walk at 10:00 a.m. With the five miles in the afternoon, the total was sixteen miles today. Everyone was right; July in Mississippi is hot, hot, hot. That is why I wake early and walk before dawn and go late until dark.

Sheryl was concerned as I had started getting a blister on one foot and my feet were swelling. She said, "I can hardly wait for Sunday so you can be off."

We checked into a hotel in Vicksburg, Mississippi, for one night and a brief morning rest. Vicksburg was the scene of one of the most prolonged battles of the American Civil War. This day, July 4, 2014, was the 151st anniversary of the end of that horrible battle. In the afternoon we visited the site of the Vicksburg siege as they were reenacting the battle, a great way to pay tribute to our fallen soldiers on both sides who fought for causes in which they believed. Later, we toured some of the old mansions of the city.

From the spring of 1862 until July 1863, Union forces waged a campaign to take the Confederate stronghold of Vicksburg, Mississippi, which lay on the east bank of the Mississippi River halfway between

Memphis and New Orleans. The capture of Vicksburg divided the Confederacy and proved the military genius of Union General Ulysses S. Grant.

Grant found the Confederates well entrenched. His army constructed fifteen miles of trenches and enclosed Confederate General Pemberton's force of 29,000 men inside the perimeter. It was only a matter of time before Grant, with 70,000 troops, captured Vicksburg. Pemberton surrendered on July 4, 1863.

Many defeated cities of the South long held grudges for the "War of Northern Aggression," and the town of Vicksburg did not celebrate the Fourth of July until 1944.

Chapter 6

Relationships Matter

*Truth is everybody is going to hurt you;
you just gotta find the ones worth suffering for.*
—Bob Marley

July 5, 2014

I WAS EXCITED TO WRAP up my walk for the week as I'll enjoy nearly forty hours of rest after walking this morning. These few minutes in the cool air before daybreak, sipping my coffee and communing with the Lord, was a treasured time. I heard a rooster crow somewhere and listened to the birds chirping in a tree just a few feet away.

At 5:40 a.m., Sheryl dropped me at MM 68 to begin the day. My goal was to end the day at MM 80. The sky was beginning to lighten, and the early-morning air was fresh and cool. "Thank you, Lord, for a few cool hours," I prayed. As the sun began its beautiful ascent over the eastern horizon, my early pace was brisk, probably a good four miles in the first hour. By the second hour, my pace slowed.

This morning the Lord urged me to focus on the nature of my relationships with other people. I wrote in my notebook, "My relationships with family and friends have been conditional." This life pattern needs attention and improvement.

Troy Waugh

Today's Reflections

A pattern of broken relationships litters my past. Divorces, harsh firings of employees, fights, arguments, and throwaway relationships are a part of my history.

Today I thought and prayed about the relationships in my life. Many of my childhood memories revolve around painful relationships with family members and others. While I am certain the good times outnumbered the bad, the harsh times are chiseled into my memory. Those events set the tone for my early difficulty with relationships. As I have matured, the quality of my relationships has improved gradually as I have invested in them.

Early family dynamics, being the target of bullying, and an addiction to work robbed me of the sense of who I was and the value of those closest to me. Until I was nearly fifty, I viewed relationships as disposable and conditional. My drive to achieve molded in me a powerful, dominant, and opinionated personality without a solid identity.

I had a horrible habit of speaking over people and finishing their sentences. Many people said nothing, including my family members, but inside they resented my dominant approach. Not hearing someone out is the height of disrespect. I'd like to tell you my view of relationships made an abrupt change for the better, but it has been gradual.

Even the greatest among us have regrets but can change. The incredible Billy Graham, evangelist and pastor to presidents, kings, and nations, shared his regrets a few years ago in his biography, *Just As I Am*.

> Although I have much to be grateful for as I look back over my life, I also have many regrets. I have failed many times, and I would do many things differently. For one thing, I would speak less and study more, and I would spend more time with my family. I would also spend more time in spiritual nurture, seeking to grow closer to God so I could become more like Christ. I would spend more time in prayer, not just for myself but for others. I would spend more time studying the Bible and meditating on its truth, not only for sermon preparation but to apply its message to my life. It is far too easy for someone in my position to read the Bible only with an eye on a future sermon, overlooking the message God has for me through its pages. And I would

give more attention to fellowship with other Christians, who could teach me and encourage me (and even rebuke me when necessary).

In my late forties and early fifties, I began to reevaluate my life's priorities. When I was fifty, I said I was in midlife. Brian said, "That's right, Dad, if you're going to live to one hundred." My mortality riveted into focus, and I had to reconsider what really mattered.

Jesus told us to "Love the Lord your God with all your heart, and with all your soul and with all your mind. This is the first and greatest commandment. The second is like it, Love your neighbor as yourself" (Matt. 22:36–40). These commandments are all about relationships: vertical with God and horizontal with neighbors. In other words, the way we are connected to God is the way we are connected to other people. There is spirituality in relationship.

※

In May 1972, my delightful second son, Brian, was born.

From 1992 to 2000, I experienced one of the most profound relationship losses of my life—estrangement with my son Brian. Experiencing the devastating loss I felt during those eight years further impressed upon me the value of relationships and the cavalier manner with which I had dealt with my family, friends, and coworkers.

Brian Allen was a gentle, loving soul from his birth. He loved his brother, his parents, his grandparents, and his friends. He won the hearts of everyone.

Since the age of six, Brian had grown to be nearly the size of Brad, who is twenty-two months older; many people thought they were twins. Brian was imbued with an incredible memory for detail. Along with this awesome memory, Brian also developed a great sensitivity and empathy for other people.

Brian was quick-witted and fun loving and shared my adventure and curiosity genes. He played junior pro football, wrestled, and played drums in the marching band and bass guitar in his performance band. He liked building and repairing things. Like me, he had an affinity for pushing the rules. One night after an argument, Brian said in his prayers, "Dear God, please don't give Daddy any more children. He doesn't know how to treat the ones he has."

Brian's IQ is comparable to Brad's, but his intelligence manifested in different ways. While Brad could study and test well, Brian struggled with reading and taking tests. He preferred listening, interacting with people, and developing his manual skills. While his mom or I would help with his homework to prepare him for tests, he would often freeze up and be unable to perform well while actually taking the tests.

Brian was around fourteen when Carolyn and I divorced. He initially lived with me while Brad lived with his mother. As are all teenagers, Brian was a challenge. I loved having Brian live with me, and we had great fun taking trips, going to movies, and breaking wind together. However, when I remarried in 1988, my new wife was abusive toward Brian, and I allowed it—a huge mistake on my part.

Carolyn moved to Washington, DC, to work for a congressman, and Brian completed his senior year at West Potomac High School in Alexandria, Virginia. Upon graduation, he enrolled in Belmont University for a year or so, transferred to Middle Tennessee State University for another year, then dropped out to work full time for FedEx.

When Brian was twenty, his world came crashing down on him. He quit school, his girlfriend walked out on him, and FedEx laid him off. The stress was too much, and he experienced a horrible mental breakdown. During the next few years, doctors misdiagnosed Brian's issue. Then finally, after more than ten years, they landed on Bipolar II Disorder. Once they correctly diagnosed Brian and provided the wonder drug needed, his mental state leveled out. For the last fifteen years, Brian's life has stabilized and he has resumed and maintained his work with FedEx for over 25 years.

Brian married Nicole Braughman in 2015, and they seem to be very happy.

In about 1990, my relationship with the Lord began to deepen. As I began to study the Bible, intimacy with God became my goal in life. I wanted to go beyond simply believing God exists and obeying—I wanted to share the joy of a relationship with the One who created the universe.

As my relationship with God deepened, so did my relationship with other people. Spiritual renewal came as I participated in three accountability or support groups: a monthly couples Bible study, Praying Men of Leiper's Fork (who called me every Friday morning as I walked), and my weekly All-In Christian Leadership Concepts (CLC) group.

John Wesley had such a group at Oxford University. He and his friends met so methodically that the other students at Oxford ridiculed them by calling them "methodists." Billy Graham had a group that worked together for over fifty years and included George Beverly Shea, Cliff Barrows, Ted Smith, and Grady Wilson. The New Testament gives evidence that Jesus had such a support group: Peter, James, and John.

During my navy stint, college years, and work with PwC and Advantage, I mostly viewed people as disposable. If they couldn't help me meet my goals, then I moved on. I had contacts, not friends or relationships. The way I had defined success was way out of focus. Looking back now, I understand I had an addiction to the urgent and was obsessed by money and power.

In 1996, a friend took me through an exercise to determine my real priorities in life. He asked me to write down at least ten things that I wanted to do, ten things I wanted to have, and ten things I wanted to be before I died—in other words, my bucket list. When we distilled the list down to the five most important things out of the thirty, all five had to do with relationships.

When I realized I had invested time into priorities that were low on my bucket list and ignored important relationships, I committed to changing, to becoming a better leader, and to strengthening relationships.

Studies show what makes people happy is having positive relationships with the people around them, people they love, care for, and respect. Living with negative relationships has disastrous effects on personal health, happiness, and life expectancy. Good relationships based on respect and trust are essential to our well-being. Networking does not work when we engage with people only when we need something from them.

I just praise God that even with the broken relationships in my history, He gave me a new life and He continues to work in me today.

<hr />

Pushing hard to cover eighty miles in six days took its toll on my legs, knees, and hips. I ached all over. That last mile of the day was all uphill on a road surface the sun had heated to nearly ninety degrees. I felt exhausted.

Sheryl was like an oasis waiting for me as I literally fell into our Tahoe. Wrapping a cool, wet cloth around my neck, I swigged on some chocolate milk, and it tasted wonderful. Two Aleve tablets gave me promise of some pain relief soon.

God had assured me that He was not done with me yet—He would give me another opportunity to live in Him and He in me so that my worship is directed to Him for the remainder of my days.

Chapter 7

The Church and Me

I have been disappointed with the church. I do not say that as one of those negative critics who can always find something wrong. I say it as a minister of the gospel who loves the church, who was nurtured in its bosom, who has been sustained by its spiritual blessings and who will remain true to it.
—Dr. Martin Luther King, in a letter from the Birmingham jail

July 7, 2014

THE REST OVER THE WEEKEND with friends in Jackson was refreshing. Gradually awakening in stages to begin day seven, I felt like a diver slowly rising to the surface from a two-hundred-foot depth. My body lay motionless for some time, eyes closed and head throbbing. However, my mind was refreshed and eager to move into another day of reflection, confession, and redemption.

"Good morning, Lord," I proclaimed as I started my quiet time that day. Then I just shut up and listened for nearly a half hour. After listening to the Lord, I made a few cryptic notes: corporate church, Christ loved the church, power, money, and humility. Those themes formed the backbone of my reflections that day.

We drove south of Jackson to MM 80, and I began walking with renewed energy at 5:40 a.m. The sun was lingering below the horizon providing a soft glow in the heavens. The temperatures seemed milder than last week. I was refreshed and praying there would be no flat tires or other accidents. Eighty miles last week was good. I didn't want to take that for granted—that was a half-marathon daily for six days.

My stepdaughter Leanna's training and advice was paying off. She had worked with me to pace myself walking, eat additional calories, drink extra fluids throughout each day, use care with any blisters, and get plenty of rest.

Feeling strong, I wondered if could cover twenty miles today. Seventeen had been the most miles I'd walked during training in May and June, so that would be a personal best.

Yesterday David Keedy, a Navy SEAL and friend, wrote me this encouraging note:

> I remember Hell Week seemed so overwhelming if I thought about in terms of "an entire week" or "six days." What helped me was to break it down into smaller pieces so I just focused on getting through one evolution at a time. At some point even that became difficult so I broke it down further to the point of literally "just put one foot in front of the other."

Today's Reflections

From my earlier prayer time, I was led to focus on my relationship with the church. Based on my limited reading of history, Christian church practices have veered away from Jesus's plan. Perhaps we should consider changing it back to serving and praising Him in small groups. Many big churches are entertainment venues and are places to see and be seen. Some Christians have already abandoned the megachurch. You can witness that across Europe and the northeastern portion of the US, where large churches have been sold or are nearly empty.

While there have been some solid Christian worshipers, inspiring gospel messages, and worship music, some of my experiences in large churches have been very disappointing. Some are "consumer churches" where people go for what they can take away or to be entertained.

I am reminded of the wife who one day after church asked her husband, "Did you see that dress Ms. Jones had on?"

Husband: "Why, no."

Wife: "Well, did you see those shoes Ms. Smith was wearing?"
Husband, a little annoyed: "No, I didn't."
Wife: "Well, what good is it for you to go to church?"

People in churches have tried to sell me insurance, investments, cars, real estate, multilevel marketing schemes, books, CDs, videos, and much more. I've even witnessed some who network at one church, then move to another "target-rich environment." Financial professionals know when a person passes away there will likely be money, insurance, or other financial matters needing attention. As a business assignment, they rotate "funeral duty." The assigned representative feigns sadness and empathy while slipping business cards to members of the grieving family at the funeral with the caveat, "If you need anything, let me know."

Some worship the pastor more than God. If the pastor leaves, they leave. In other situations, the people in the church look down on "those heathens" in other churches but shoot their wounded rather than help them heal.

I am not saying we should give up on church, just return it to the small groups of people worshiping God and supporting each other. Many of the churches I have attended don't look anything like those described in the Bible. The early church didn't own property. There were no denominations, no megachurches, and no dues or apportionments. There was a spirit of community and bonding among the people.

The first Christians met together regularly, sold their possessions, and shared with those in need. They met in homes and shared their meals. Each day the Lord added to their group those who were being saved (Acts 2:44–47). People were not forced by the state to share everything—the Christians did so willingly.

The state-sponsored religious leaders were threatened by the believers, so they began persecuting Christians. That persecution brought the Christians closer to one another. In the fourth century, Constantine issued the Edict of Milan, which made Christianity legal throughout the Roman Empire. The community-based house churches became land-owning, building-filling congregations. Land and buildings needed funding, managers, and care, so a professional class of paid clergy and managers arose. As a growth culture developed for these institutional churches, the leaders of the larger churches had more prestige than the smaller ones. Soon the focus on Jesus was replaced with a focus on the corporate goal of getting larger, raising more funds, hiring staff members, and cooperating with the state.

A focus on bigger churches, owning land, mega-buildings, corporate growth, and entertainment is the norm today. The expression of Jesus's presence in the world has turned into a religious corporation.

The modern American church allies itself with power and money and has taken on aspects of the marketplace with bookstores, coffee shops, gyms, sports teams, budgets, salaries, hierarchies, promotion, publicity, politics, mega-buildings, and on and on. Jesus's anger at this type of activity was demonstrated when he tipped over the tables of the money changers in the temple.

When I get discouraged about the state of the church, then I look to see God at work in people serving Him in numerous ways and I praise Him.

Sheryl's Notes

Troy needed to eat before his walk, so he found a McDonald's open. I still do not think he is eating or drinking enough. I want him to take care of himself; he is so special to me and so many others. When I was single, I asked God to send me a good Christian man. You know the rest. God sent me Troy. I am blessed!

This morning, the temperature was wonderful, but traffic was terrible. I am so shocked how many cars use the trace in Jackson. I worry about Troy getting hit! Thank you, God, for the bright T-shirts he wears! Due to the traffic, he felt it unsafe for me to pull off on the side of the road every half mile, so I had to promise to go to the pull-off designated for parking. I hated doing this, but I knew he was right. I just feel best being near him in case of emergency. I had to drive ahead of him about four miles to the next pull-off, and I did not like this idea.

A suburb of Jackson, Clinton is a little town with the historical district consisting of a few stores, mostly antique shops. I first stopped at the Clinton Visitor Center, the prettiest visitor's center I have been to. The landscaping was so beautiful my garden club would appreciate it! I sat on the front porch rocking while listening to the birds sing, taking

The Church and Me

in the beauty as I waited patiently for it to open so I could get a restroom key.

A car pulled in, and a cute little white-haired lady hopped out and quickly headed to the door with keys. She looked to be about eighty, but she really had bounce in her step. Her makeup was on nicely, her hair fluffy, and earrings matched her outfit.

Within the first minute she had probably asked five questions. She had passed Troy on the trace, so she and her two helpers wanted to know all about why he was walking. They also wanted to be sure I knew everything about the visitor's center and their little town. They were so proud.

While I waited for Troy to finish, I rolled the windows up, turned the motor off, locked the doors, and napped! Troy and I texted about every thirty minutes, and I went back to sleep. All of a sudden someone pecked on the glass. It was Troy who had caught up with me!

I moved on ahead to the next safe rest area, prayed, and waited. I didn't have to wait long. I looked way down the road and saw a little yellowish-green spot—my honey and his bright shirt! He was absolutely exhausted after thirteen miles of dodging cars and wading knee-high weeds. He had to move into the weeds to avoid the cars.

No matter how uncomfortable my life can be, there is no comparison with what the homeless go through. It makes me feel uncomfortable not having a nearby restroom, having to eat in restaurants without home-cooked meals, and missing our family, friends, and home. But this discomfort is nothing compared to living on the streets, sleeping on concrete, eating from dumpsters, and not having family.

I ask myself, How can I touch a homeless person's life in a positive way each day? Can I serve meals, furnish soap, sit and listen to their stories, and help them feel important? If each of us could do one thing it will make a difference.

Today I am witness to the work of Jesus being carried out by many small parachurch ministries. Community Care Fellowship is just one such ministry. Founded in 1984 by my friend Ken Powers and his wife, Carol, the team at CCF ministers to the poor and homeless of our community by providing meals, hygiene services, shelter, tutoring, and job and medical referrals. Ken has passed away, but I had the undeserved good fortune of knowing and working with him for about twenty years and am a witness to the impact his life has had for generations after his physical death. He was a mentor and friend and an example of how the Lord can change our lives in dramatic ways.

Ken was a retired US Army officer and political writer. Together we conceived and launched a new magazine in 1982, *Tennessee Business*, just prior to his launching CCF.

Ken always had a heart for Jesus and the homeless. In his free time, he and Carol, helped the homeless survive on the rough streets of our city. In 1983, he came to me one day and said, "I can't stand it anymore. God has been calling me to full-time ministry with the homeless, and I can't deny His calling on my life." He left our company, and at age fifty-five went back to Emory University for his divinity degree. After being ordained as a Methodist minister, he began walking the streets and pulling drunks out of alleys. He found shelter for homeless people, got resources and medical care for the poor and sick, and ministered in the way he had heard the call of Jesus. The ministry goes on today providing the love of Jesus, just as Ken and Carol did when they built the ministry over thirty-five years ago.

I've written a poem about Ken Powers that chronicles his life of ministry to the needy:

Brother Ken

"Hi, Brother Ken."
"Hello, Bear."
I stop and stare.
What did you say?
Who was he? Why do you care?

We're in our corporate suits.
Bear lives under the bridge,
Has a scruffy beard,
Tattered hat, dirty jeans, worn-out boots.
But a big warm smile for Brother Ken.

He comes to the shelter at lunch.
The homeless, a maudlin bunch,
Many are bipolar, schizophrenic, and diseased.
Brains fried on alcohol and drugs,
We can't keep them locked up;
The government wants them released.

Knowing the odds are poor
Of saving these souls,
Dealing with vomit and stench
And the indescribable scent of Satan.
Day after day, oh how I wish
The muck and the gore,
The druggies and whores,
The sick and the lame
Could be well and pure and clean.

But God has called Ken to love, yield, and obey.
Ken didn't choose it this way.
"But when I am serving, my soul is full;
The Spirit guides me."
I dreamed that life was happiness;
I learned that life is service.
I have discovered that service is joy. Makes me complete.
Connects my soul to God and God has fulfilled my joy.

Some men find peace in beaches and golf.
Some never find their deep gifts.
I think when Brother Ken is feeding the poor,
This is love beyond understanding.
This is pure, true love.
This joy is what Brother Ken lived his life for.

Private Pain and Public Sorrow

Sheryl and I stayed in Jackson, Mississippi, over the weekend and had dinner one evening with Sheryl's niece, Kathy Ann Barnhill. Kathy's story is an amazing story of redemption and renewal. From a life of confusion, Kathy turned her life around and became a medical professional—a cardiac surgery center perfusionist.

After dinner on Saturday evening, we met Kathy's eighty-year-old friend and his fifty-year-old son. Everyone seemed in ebullient spirits. The son told us that his farm adjoined the eastern edge of the Natchez Trace Parkway. I joked that I would wave at him as I walked by. He and his father seemed jovial, without any unusual care in the world.

The next day Sheryl and I were stunned when we learned that this young man had committed suicide. We were so saddened as we prayed about this man, his father, and Kathy. I wondered how someone could come to the point of his private pain becoming unbearable. He must not have had anyone in whom to confide his misery or a personal relationship with Jesus so he could be healed and loved.

When I walked by the location of his farm and looked across the fields, I thought about him ending his life behind locked doors, and I forgave him for walking out on his father. It may be futile to try to understand why anyone would pull the trigger that ends it all, as it makes no sense.

Today as I walked into the southern suburbs of Jackson, the interstate traffic forced me to the shoulder from about MM 86 to 93 in the morning and from MM 93 to 100 in the afternoon. My day's walk was almost five hours in the morning, from 5:45 until 10:40, and then a bit over two hours in the evening, from 5:45 p.m. until 8:00. God gave me the strength to walk the twenty miles I had hoped for today—my best yet.

Chapter 8

What Is Love?

Don't force me to leave you; don't make me go home. Where you go, I go; and where you live, I'll live. Your people are my people, your God is my god; where you die, I'll die, and that's where I'll be buried, so help me GOD—not even death itself is going to come between us!
—Ruth 1:16–17 MSG

July 8, 2014

TUESDAY, I WAS AWAKE BEFORE the alarm rang, eagerly into communion with the Lord and feeling prepared to step out in faith. I started off my quiet time with the Lord by saying something like, "Lord, you have filled my mind with extraordinary thoughts of you. Yet my mind is nowhere near as tired as my body. You are stretching my mind and my soul." God calmed me down with the thought that our minds and souls are eternally expanding aspects of our beings. I sensed the Lord wanted me to focus on the nature of love.

At 5:50 a.m., Sheryl drove me to begin my day at MM 100. The sun touched the horizon as I bowed to God with a prayer of thanks for the new day, for the trees, lake, grass, and all His creation. God had given me a mission, and I was excited about talking with Him, witnessing the beauty of the morning sunrise, and walking.

Yesterday was an awesome day, and I felt exhilarated over covering twenty miles to the north side of Jackson. Contending with the traffic was a little unnerving at times, but my energy level and enthusiasm was tip-top.

When people heard I was walking the trace, some asked, "Where will you sleep? At camping sites?"

My response usually was something like, "The walk will be difficult enough, so I will stay in bed and breakfasts or motels along the way." Others mentioned I should consider the Appalachian Trail or Camino de Santiago in Spain.

My response was, "Let me get through this and see what God has in store."

Sheryl found a service called Natchez Trace Travel to plan our overnight stays.[1] Randy Fought built this website as a service for people moving up and down the trace, walking, running, motorcycling, bicycling, or driving. He offers an excellent selection of B and B's and small independent motels along the way.

At first I thought I could map out my trip plan and make reservations weeks ahead, but I quickly learned that my daily mileage was unpredictable. We had to cancel the reservations I made beyond the first week. After that, we made a reservation a day or two ahead and were still able to get good rooms at reasonable rates.

My friend Brad Preber of Phoenix, Arizona, sent me another encouraging note today:

> I admire your drive and wish you Godspeed. This is a walk about things much bigger than one's self. You are bringing attention to important issues that need our resources. In addition, you are learning about yourself and how fragile and imperfect one can be when forced to deal with the unknown and unplanned.
>
> Rise above these circumstances. See the irony around the situations you are encountering and the discomfort you are feeling. This is what the homeless deal with every day. Your walk is a remarkable shadow of their lives. Each step forward is progress toward hope.
>
> "Those who hope in the Lord will renew their strength. They will soar on wings like eagles, they will run and not grow weary, they will walk and not be faint" (Isa. 40:31).

---

[1] https://www.natcheztracetravel.com.

Reach inside to find your inner sprit. It will give you peace and strength beyond your physical body. In the altered words of the great film Forrest Gump: "Walk, Troy! Walk."

Within a couple of hours, Jackson's city traffic lessened as I approached the Ross Barnett Reservoir just to the east of the trace. The 33,000-acre reservoir, named for a former governor of Mississippi, provides habitat for wildlife and recreation for thousands of people. While the temperature approached ninety, there was a slight breeze off the lake. Thank you, Jesus.

Today's Reflections

Today I am reflecting on the concept of love. What does it mean? How is it expressed? The subject of countless poems, books, and songs, love is used as both a word with deep meaning and a throw away. We say, "I love chocolate. I love the color blue. I love the smell of vanilla. I love my dog. I love my mother. I love my wife. I love my child. Love makes the world go round. I love Jesus. I love you."

Perhaps I still don't know what love is. I've read about it in books and listened to songs that try to explain the meaning of love. I've heard songs that say love is like a river, like an undying flame, or like a warm breeze. How can love be so many different things yet be one thing?

Love is one of the best feelings in the world, without question. We fall into it, seek it out, cherish it, share it. It's an experience and expression everyone can understand, no matter what language they speak or where they live. Many people hide their true selves for fear people won't love them if the real person is exposed. Many people move from one love to the next to experience the emotional high from the new love, like a drug addict needing a new fix after the old one is gone. As universal as love is, it's also a complex, powerful emotion that is hard to define. Is love something you choose? Is it something you feel? Once you find love, can it leave? Can love grow? Can love die?

Loving Self

In boot camp, a chaplain asked my company of new recruits, "Who do you love the most?" At this point in boot camp (six weeks) every guy was feeling homesickness and aloneness. When he posed that question, the answers came back, "My mother," "My girlfriend," and "My parents." One guy shouted out, "I love sleep."

I sensed the chaplain had a deeper motive so I answered "Me." The chaplain then said loving self is the greatest of all human loves for most people. To care for others, we must first learn to care for ourselves. This self-love is not the unhealthy, self-obsessed, narcissistic kind.

The chaplain told us once you have the strength to love yourself, you will be able to love others. He introduced me to Jesus's words, "Love the Lord your God with all your heart and with all your soul and with all your mind and with all your strength. The second is this: Love your neighbor as yourself" (Mark 12:30–31).

He pointed out that all sin derives from an all-consuming love of self so one has little space to love anyone else.

You cannot share what you do not have. If you do not love yourself, you cannot love anyone else. On the other hand, our tendency toward self-absorption seems to stop with the command to love self. If love stops at self, it quickly becomes self-indulgence. For many, the quest for self-love is never ending and all consuming.

The chaplain quoted the Scripture, "Greater love no man has than this, to lay down his life for his friends" (John 15:13). He said volunteering for service to our country indicated we were risking our lives on behalf of our families, friends, and countrymen. He encouraged us to seek God's guidance in our lives during our naval service and to love Him with all our hearts to be happy and fulfilled.

Here are a few loving words from the woman I love:

Sheryl's Notes

It's so pretty this morning watching the sun come up over the water just north of Jackson. The trace goes by the Ross Barnett Reservoir, and I found a pull-off that sits high above the water, so the view is wonderful. It would be outstanding to have an antebellum home sitting here. I can see Miss Scarlett now! The breeze is blowing nicely over the water while the birds sing happy songs. God's precious blessings.

Troy did great yesterday! Twenty miles in one day! He hopes to do the same today, and this will lighten his load for the end of the week. He has a goal of ninety miles per week.

I think this trip is not only for the homeless. God is

teaching me a few lessons along the way. One is to stop and smell the roses. The other is that I do not always have to have my makeup on and hair fixed when going out the door! We can all slow our pace down and not focus on self as I often have. We need to thank God and listen to what he has in mind for us. When I get home, one thing I will definitely make time for is doing more for the people who are in need. I promised God when I retired I would do more and have, but I can do much more!

I would like to challenge each of you who is retired or isn't working outside the home to set aside at least a half a day a week to help someone else. It could be to feed the homeless at the mission, visit an elderly person and brighten their day, cook for someone who is sick, or volunteer at the children's hospital. If we start small and just do one thing and repeat it at least three times, it could become a habit. I would like to have a big basket like Goldilocks had, filled with goodies to give to ones in need.

Wouldn't it be awesome to go to the nursing home and polish the little ladies' nails? When I worked, it always made me feel so good to help the ladies who came in struggling with health issues like cancer. I always gave them hope, for without hope where would we be? I listened to their stories and I hugged them because I cared. Whatever you choose to be your mission, be sure you have a passion for it. With passion, your goodness will shine. Look around and see how you can add sunshine to a gloomy day in a person's life.

Mature Love

A few weeks ago, I ran into Coach Bob Cummings, an old friend of mine. He's ninety-two years old and is a very happy man who's gained great wisdom through his years. His first wife passed away, and he is now married to Emmie, whom he adores.

"What's the real meaning of love, Bob?" I asked.

He looked at me seriously. I could see he was tapping into the emotion of his marriages, and he told me something that I will always remember.

"Troy, you know you're in love when you can't wait to come home; you have a reason to look forward. You'll know you're in love when you can't imagine living without her. You'll do anything to be with her and to protect her. You cannot see this kind of love; you cannot touch this kind of love. You cannot explain it or define it, but it makes you want to wake up tomorrow."

Bob, with his years of wisdom, made sense. I so admire the choices of wise and mature individuals, like my mother and father, who kept the covenant of marriage sacred for a lifetime.

Bob and Emmie have a love that has matured and deepened over time. It is beyond the physical, it has transcended the casual, and it is a unique harmony of two lives.

This kind of love is found in married couples who've been together for a long time or in friendships that span decades. It's found between people who've learned to make compromises and have demonstrated patience and tolerance to make their love work over the long haul. Many people spend so much time and energy chasing new love and so little time learning how to maintain it that their love does not endure.

Romantic Love

It is hard to describe the intense, overwhelming feeling of a new romantic love. When I fell in love as a boy, I felt giddy and stupid. I wanted to spend all my time with my girlfriend and could think of no one else but her. I was experiencing the feelings of the early stages of falling in love with someone—the fluttering heart, flirting, teasing, and feelings of euphoria. It was so overwhelming and new.

Having experienced three marriages of nineteen years, seventeen years, and now eight years, I can attest to the euphoria of the early relationship.

When I met my first wife, I experienced a deeper love than I knew was possible. It was a combination of romantic and erotic love. Simultaneously and right away, this love felt wonderful, dangerous, and frightening. It involved a loss of control through a passionate and intense form of love that aroused vulnerable romantic and sexual feelings.

Over time, I learned erotic love is a primal and powerful fire that requires discipline to keep alive. It needs its flame to be fanned through deeper forms of love as it is centered among the selfish aspects of love, including personal infatuation and physical pleasure. Frankly, I was not mature enough to handle the long-term covenant of love. Mine was misguided, misused, abused, and indulged in, which led to impulsive acts and broken hearts.

Unconditional Love

The love parents have for children endures no matter what the child may do. The love a father has for one child is different than the love for another child. It's not a matter of favorites but is unique between each parent and each child.

The Greeks called this *storge*. It symbolizes a great and enduring love, a love without conditions. They say when your first grandchildren arrive, you find out what true love really is. It's a bond that goes deeper than blood. It's the union of two generations that leaves a lasting emotional mark. There's nothing more satisfying than being a grandchild, then later in life being a grandparent.

Upon the arrival of grandchildren, the relationship between parents and children changes. Differences shrink and ties are strengthened in this new stage of the life cycle.

I have five grandchildren, and each is unique. My first grandchild is Brian's son, David, now in college. David and I have a special bond as at times I have served as his surrogate father. Max, Brad's son, has the leadership qualities one would expect from a firstborn. Brad and Tara's twins, Miles and Maya, are different as night and day. Then Daniel, Leanna's stepson, has stolen our hearts as well.

Friendship

Friendship is a love without erotic overtones and is considered a love between equals. This type of love often involves feelings of loyalty among friends, camaraderie among teammates, and the sense of sacrifice for your buddies. Most of us have very few of these close friends.

Is there a person in your life you haven't seen for a few years but who could call you and ask you for help with your response being a quick yes? That is such a friend.

Divine Love

The deepest and most profound type of love is selfless, *agape*. This is the type of love that Paul is talking about in 1 Corinthians 13. This love has nothing to do with the condition-based love our sex-obsessed culture tries to pass off as love. It is an unconditional love bigger than we are; a love that is pure. It is intentional love, free from conditions or expectations. It exists regardless of the shortcomings of another. Agape is that love to which we aspire in order to be aligned with God's love. That is how He loves us. It is a spiritual, boundless, infinite love. Agape is divine love.

God granted the covenant of marriage to incorporate all these types of love. He made marriage the holiest relationship. In that relationship, all forms of love must thrive for the marriage to survive. With romantic or erotic love alone, no marriage will pass the test of time.

When I ponder how God loves me, how He is constantly with me, constantly guiding me, and providing for me, I wonder if my love can ever measure up?

Sheryl, My Love

When I divorced in 2005, I vowed never to remarry. The emotional drain was too hard to risk bearing again. The night Sheryl and I met in September of 2009, I remarked to my sister, "I may have met someone who will change my mind about marriage."

Sheryl was a good businesswoman, having established and run a very successful hair-replacement institute for women and children. She raised four girls and loved each one of them deeply. Sheryl is a very outgoing but humble person. While she is a beauty on the outside, the depth of her inner beauty is limitless.

We began dating, and within a few months I fell in love with her, and we were married in September 2010.

The youngest of seven children, Sheryl grew up on a farm in Hickman County, Tennessee. She has twin brothers and four older sisters. As her sisters married and moved away from the farm, she dreamed of having her own family, children, a home, and a job. As a little girl, she often created various home layouts and designs in the forest near her home.

Sheryl adored her father, Spencer Ferguson, who was a cattle farmer and music leader in their small church. She loved to ride with him to buy cattle or just to roam the backcountry roads and talk.

Sheryl's mother was responsible for raising seven children on almost no money. As a Depression-era woman, Pearl Ferguson demonstrated how to scrimp and save and make do with very little. Sheryl often visited with her older sisters, Beverly and Jan, in their homes. It was as if she had several mothers who loved her.

Sheryl has unique skills in working with people. As a teenager, she began working in a beauty shop, washing hair and cleaning the floors. While her dad and brothers helped finance her education, she worked to help send herself to beauty school and had a job cutting and styling hair before she was twenty. Over forty-plus years, Sheryl built her hairstyling business into a thriving hair-replacement enterprise that employed a dozen professionals. She invented an innovative procedure to provide natural-looking hair especially for women and children who were dealing with scalp disorders and/or the side effects of cancer treatments.

After she married Robert, Sheryl instantly became the mother of three stepdaughters, for whom she has a genuine love. She always wanted a large family. The desire of her heart was to birth a child herself, and after years of medical treatment, she had the baby of her dreams—Leanna. Sheryl doted on her baby girl and worked hard to provide her an education, clothing, food, and shelter.

Sheryl picked me up about 10:30, and I enjoyed a cool beer in the car to build back my carbs. We returned to the motel, and after a brief rest, we had lunch and took in a movie.

Then it was back on the trace from 6:00 to 8:00 p.m. to complete another twenty-mile day. Walking in the evening as the sun was setting in the west was much different than in the early morning. The air felt tired and the humidity heavy. The mosquitoes buzzing around my ears were searching for one more bite before nightfall. After about 7:00 p.m., the deer were prancing out of the forest and across the road with no fear. They seemed fully aware they are protected in this national park. As the cover of darkness spread across the land, I began to praise God. What a great and awesome day walking with a great and awesome God.

Chapter 9

The Power of the Holy Spirit

*Self-control is not control by oneself through one's
own willpower but rather control of oneself
through the power of the Holy Spirit.*
—Jerry Bridges, *Holiness Day by Day: Transformational
Thoughts for Your Spiritual Journey*

July 9, 2014

Sheryl is so good to get up, help with breakfast, and have us to the trace to MM 120 by 5:50. On this day, she decided to stay close. What a trooper she is!

We moved yesterday from Jackson to Canton, Mississippi, for a couple of nights. To conserve energy and go into the weekend with strength, I will intentionally back off the mileage.

A few miles north of Ross Barnett Lake, I entered the Cypress Swamp Hike area. It reminds me of something you'd see around the Everglades—all green, slimy, and the air heavy with moisture. It felt in any moment that a creature might come out of the swamp to greet me. The bald cypress and water tupelo trees line the edges of the parkway. The water tupelos rise over ninety feet, and the bald cypress, in order to aerate, have knees that grow up out of the swampland.

If your idea of the Deep South is Spanish moss swaying in a slight breeze over swampy marshes where alligators and snakes glide, this is where your dreams meet reality. Crossing the wooden footbridge into the swamp, I entered a quiet, watery world populated by giant bullfrogs, water moccasins, otters, and turtles.

My senses were stirred by the variety and beauty of this Central Mississippi natural landscape. The early-morning sun rays poked through the branches and leaves like laser beams from heaven. The trees seemed to be whispering, *Stay awhile and rest in our world.*

For much of my life, I have taken the beauty and holiness of nature for granted. I have been so concerned with the hustle and bustle of business, that I have sometimes been oblivious to the wonders of nature. This morning on the trace I became deeply aware of the abundance of the voices of the lakes, trees, swamps, birds, frogs, clouds, rain, and flowers. As nature's voices surrounded me, I also wanted to hear the breath of God whisper to me. I loved walking in this place and felt so welcome.

Sheryl believes nature is constantly telling us about the condition of heart and soul, our inner selves, and the quality of life here and now. She has formed a pathway to God through nature and believes that nature makes us aware of the preciousness of life.

Today's Reflections

During my quiet time, the Lord simply seemed to whisper something like, "Go with it today. Enjoy what I have in store for you." Every other day of my walk, God gave me clear instructions on my reflections for that day. Having a definite purpose fits my personality, so going without an agenda caused me some discomfort. I determined to lean into the Lord and trust Him as the day unfolded.

Over the last twenty years, I have worked on my listening power—particularly with the Spirit of God. During my prayers, God becomes present as I hear the Spirit, who then directs, corrects, and encourages. When Jesus ascended to heaven, He told the disciples He would not leave them alone but would send the Holy Spirit. The Holy Spirit is the breath of God. The fullness of God's presence is revealed in the Holy Spirit.

The words I've heard from the Spirit have not been words to apply to someone else later, but words for me to obey here and now. Today I pondered how God comes to us as we listen.

Romans 8:14 tells us the Holy Spirit leads us in our everyday lives.

More and more as I have matured in my personal relationship with the Lord, His Spirit prompts me in what I should do. At times these promptings are unclear whispers if I have been so out of touch with the Spirit that I cannot hear or understand His quiet words. However, there is no question the Holy Spirit is always tugging and leading me.

My initial reaction when I have a personal encounter with the Spirit is not to broadcast it but rather to savor it, let it sink in, enquire of it, and gather its full meaning. Due to the noise and distractions of life, God's work may go unnoticed. I am uncertain how to tell others about my encounters with God. I want to be careful not to distort the truth by identifying God with an event or circumstance. God is divine and cannot be fully understood by the human mind, and my relationship with God is sacred to me.

People often say, "It was a God thing." People on both sides of a contest count on God to help them win. But no Christian, pastor, priest, Jew, or rabbi has any special knowledge about God. God cannot be limited by any human level of understanding. He is greater than our minds and hearts and perfectly free to reveal himself wherever and whenever He chooses. I believe our job is to praise Him, thank Him, and do our part to love Him.

When I heard the Holy Spirit speaking to me back in May, I held it close for two weeks. The urging became stronger each day. During those two weeks the Lord confirmed that He would provide a divine healing of my soul. There is no way I could have grasped the depth and breadth of the encounter these months have provided as I've been alone with nature and the Lord.

Kevin, a brother of one of our friends, has been struggling with terminal cancer. As we have watched him decline, we have prayed daily and earnestly for Kevin and his family. We prayed that God would heal his cancer and allow him to live a long life and see his grandchildren and their children. This morning we received word that Kevin may be in his last hours. Were we going to be disappointed if God takes Kevin home? Would we be unhappy with God? What would our reaction be if God does not give us the thing for which we pray?

Sheryl had parked the Tahoe a few miles ahead. When she spotted me coming, she began walking south toward me. She had been praying. I had been praying. We were encountering God in the Cypress Swamp along the green, murky waters and bogs of Mississippi. As Sheryl came into view, I noticed a puzzled look on her face. The wind got louder the closer she got to me. When she was within one hundred yards or so, the water tupelo trees on the west side of the trace were making the sweetest music as they shook back and forth. The winds seemed to be contained in a twenty-five- or thirty-yard stretch, just three or four trees alongside where Sheryl was walking.

When we met, Sheryl said, "The wind has been following me for nearly a mile." We stopped, held hands, and experienced the Holy Spirit wash over us. Neither of us had ever experienced such a phenomenon together. Sheryl and I were with God in holy communion. We both sensed it was the Holy Spirit saying, *I have Kevin and he is going to be okay.* We later learned that it was around 10:00 a.m. on the morning of July 9 that Kevin Gernentz went home to the Lord.

Sheryl's Notes

Troy was on the trail at 5:30 this morning. We were both dragging. We had a long day yesterday, but Troy made his twenty miles and will do less today. Leanna has him build up and then slow down so he does not get overworked. He hopes to do only ten miles this morning.

The pull-offs are really spread apart, and since Troy covers a lot of territory, I move often. Early this morning I was at the Cypress Swamp pull-off. It was awesome! I walked over the bridge looking over an eerie sight of huge tall cypress trees that appeared to pop out of nowhere. The water appeared to be thick with green slime. I was expecting something to come out of the water and grab me like you see in horror movies.

I have now moved to another area and pulled off on a gravel road under trees. It is so peaceful, and the birds are very happy. The sounds are much quieter after 7:30. It is very apparent they are early morning birds, unlike me!

The Power of the Holy Spirit

I wanted to walk a little, so I parked at Cypress Swamp and started my walk toward Troy. I was praying for God to please heal Kevin Gernentz and be with his family, when out of nowhere I heard a noise sounding like a waterfall, but I realized it was not water. I looked around to see where the noise was coming from, and there were three trees clumped together making a rustling sound. All the other trees were completely still. This was the only movement out of hundreds of trees! I was thinking, Is this You, God, letting me know You heard me? I kept walking and started to pray again for Kevin and Kris. The noise started again. God's presence was very obvious to me, especially after the second time.

Sheryl and I both were overcome with emotion that we had heard from the Holy Spirit today. We called Kris, Kevin's brother, and shared our experiences and basked in the glow of God blessing our marriage.

In John 14:26, Jesus tells us the Holy Spirit will come to us and lead us into all truth. Through the whisperings of the Holy Spirit, we are able to grasp answers to some of life's issues. Without the Holy Spirit, much remains unclear. The Holy Spirit speaks to each of us in unique ways and leads us by applying God's Word to our daily lives.

That morning we had been standing on holy ground and communicating with the Holy Spirit. Over and over, the song "Holy, Holy, Holy" played in my head. The writers of the music and lyrics of the hymn, John B. Dykes and Reginald Heber, celebrated the quietness and the awesomeness of the Holy Spirit in its words.

> Holy, holy, holy! Lord God Almighty!
> Early in the morning our song shall rise to Thee.
> Holy, holy, holy! Merciful and mighty!
> God in three Persons, blessed Trinity!

> Holy, holy, holy! Lord, God Almighty!
> All Thy works shall praise Thy name in earth and sky and sea
> Holy, holy, holy! Merciful and mighty!
> God in three Persons, blessed Trinity.

Troy Waugh

We are born into the world naked, vulnerable, and weak. The mystery of service in the Lord's kingdom is that we are called to serve not with our power but with our powerlessness.

I have come to believe that the gifts of the Holy Spirit are for us to experience in our daily lives. God did not stop speaking when the Holy Bible was written.

Because I am a type A self-starter, I always try to see the big picture, the bottom line, and achieve a long list of to-dos. I have to be reminded that I am a human *being*, not a human *doing*. My work is abiding in the Lord and listening to the breath of His Holy Spirit. I have always feared waiting is being irresponsible, but that is one of the paradoxes of our Christian faith. We must rest and wait to receive power.

How many times have I said, "The only thing left to do is to pray"? I got it all backward, didn't I? Isn't looking to God for power and wisdom and direction the first thing we're supposed to be doing? Why would we dare attempt to do anything until He has made good on His promise of "power from on high"?

Why does the Holy Spirit speak so softly? Why must I slow down my pace of life and carefully attune my heart to His voice? I wish He would hit me on the head with a two-by-four sometimes. Maybe He has!

***

After only having covered ten miles, I had blistered feet and swollen ankles, so I wrapped up my walk for the day about 10:00 a.m. so I could ice to reduce the inflammation.

Chapter 10

Faith Is the Foundation

To one who has faith, no explanation is necessary.
To one without faith, no explanation is possible.
—Thomas Aquinas

July 10, 2014

WHILE WE WERE HEADING FOR the trace, thunderstorms with lightning covered the area around Canton, Mississippi, at MM 130. The rain-filled cloud ambassadors of the Lord broke open, so we returned to the hotel for three more hours of sleep. *Thank You, Lord, for the rain and the rest.* The Lord was teaching me stillness and rest. *Lord, I am walking for You, in your power. I would run for You if you ordered it. Today You are showing me I must kneel in peace, humility, and rest.*

The torrential downpour and my subsequent rest made me think of how my life has turned like a slow river away from darkness and toward light. I once indulged in pride and arrogance, grasping at a false faith in myself. Now I seek to be washed in the blood of Jesus and have faith in Him. I must diminish so He can grow in me.

God controls the weather. Is it wrong of me to think God sent that rain just for me? Over the past few days, as the cool air brushed my face, it was as if God was saying, *I'm here.* Today I praised and thanked Him for the rain.

During my normal quiet time and coffee around 5:00 a.m., my

pattern of dominant self-reliance came to my mind. Why is it I can't seem to trust other people? Does that translate into a reluctance to trust the Lord? As I examined my own faith, I admitted an overwhelming portion of my faith had been in me and not in God. From an early age, I felt I couldn't trust other people. Naturally, I learned to take matters into my own hands. During the walk today, I considered how that cycle has affected me.

Around midday, we moved to a B and B in Kosciusko, Mississippi. In the late afternoon Sheryl dropped me off at MM 130, and I hoped to cover nine miles. In an open field, two coyotes were slinking toward a buck leaping across the road. It would have required a pack to take that big boy down.

The Workingman Angel

About 7:30 p.m., a dark blue car drove past me, slowed, and turned around before stopping on the west shoulder of the road. The car was at least fifteen years old and had a dented rear fender and many rusty spots. A workingman, dirty and tired from a hard day of labor was driving. His face was round with a stubbly beard—the kind that hadn't been shaved for three days. His eyes were gentle, his jaw was firm, and his chin was angular. There were cheap baby toys in the back seat, a McDonald's wrapper on the floor, and the seat covers were torn and tattered.

"What are you doing?" he asked.

"I am walking the Natchez Trace from Natchez to Nashville."

"Why would you do such a thing?"

"God asked me to do this in order to heal myself and to raise awareness and funds for a homeless ministry in Nashville, Community Care Fellowship."

I stuck out my hand and said, "Hello, I'm Troy. What's your name?"

"I'm J. D., and I want to help with your ministry." He pulled out three one dollar bills from his wallet. Then he reached into the glove box and found two more crumpled-up dollar bills. He put them all together and handed them to me, saying, "Here, please take this to your homeless ministry. And God bless you."

I was stunned. This man gave me all the money he had in faith I would take it to CCF. He may have had more at home, but it was clear from his appearance and his car's that he was not a wealthy man. This hardworking man gave me all he had.

I thanked J. D., and we prayed for my safety and for his generosity and for the poor and homeless at CCF.

As he drove away, I felt like I had been visited by an angel. Meeting J. D. gave me renewed faith that God was with me. For the next hour, I hardly knew what I was doing as I was so stunned anyone would do this. With renewed energy, I was eager to meet the challenges of the next few miles. And I knew I would sleep better knowing God's angels were with me and caring for me. God had provided me with an indelible moment of joy by showing me He is with me in all ways on all days.

In the exquisite twilight of that summer day, I soaked it all into my soul. And the quietest voice whispered, "You are welcome."

Today's Reflections

Today the message I am hearing is *Have faith in the Lord.*

In 1975, I felt an overwhelming exhaustion that lasted for months. Total faith in myself had led me to physical, mental, and moral bankruptcy. I had little energy, gained weight, and became lethargic. Exhausted, I lacked the ability to make good choices, and I strayed from God into a life of sin and self-satisfaction—perhaps the greatest sin of all. Following the workaholic example of my father, I worked simply because it was the thing to do. With my motivation coming from money and power, I had very little reliance on the God of the universe.

Today I am committed to cultivating my faith and relying on God's direction.

Faith for Lug Nuts

Steve Lorenz and Marti Scudder are the founders of Mission Development International (MDI). A few years ago, Steve and Marti were working with an MDI client in Ukraine, Pastor Anatoly Kaluzhny. They were traveling in a van on a crowded highway with heavy trucks in front, behind, and passing on the left. Suddenly, there was a loud *clunk*, and the van shuddered. They stopped and inspected the vehicle, found everything to be in order, and resumed their trip. About five minutes later, the left rear wheel came off, and the van swerved. Fighting the wheel, Pastor Kaluzhny brought the van to a stop as the detached wheel rolled down the middle of the left side of the road.

When the van came to rest, Pastor Kaluzhny yelled, "Go get the lug nuts," as he jumped out of the van and chased the rolling wheel down the highway. Just then the traffic cleared, and there were no trucks flying by, no cars zooming past, none in front or back. Steve and Marti jumped out to look for the lug nuts. Steve looked at Marti and said, "There is no way we are going to find five lug nuts. They must be scattered for miles up the highway behind us."

Steve and Marti began to search and found one within a few minutes. Then another and another. Within about ten minutes they had found all five of the lug nuts.

Pastor Kaluzhny captured the runaway wheel. Amazingly, the roadway was still absent of congested traffic. The pastor jacked up the van, replaced the wheel, and tightened the lug nuts.

Once the van got back on the road, the heavy traffic resumed.

Steve asked Pastor Kaluzhny, "How did you know we would find the lug nuts?"

"We prayed to God for our safety, and I believed Him," he said.

Anatoly, Steve, and Marti prayed for safety before leaving on their trip, and Pastor Kaluzhny expected safety. He didn't hesitate, didn't doubt, nor did he stop to analyze the situation. He acted on faith that they would be safe—and find the lug nuts.

A Life of Faith

The Christian life *is* a life of faith, and was exhibited in a dramatic way that day.

Faith is unlike the fruit of the Spirit, such as patience and gentleness. Faith is unlike spiritual gifts, such as teaching and service; unlike spiritual disciplines, such as worship and prayer. Faith is not one part among assorted components. This true experience illustrates the kind of faith Jesus is talking about in Matthew 17: 20–21. "I tell you truth, if you have faith as small as a mustard seed, you can say to this mountain 'move from here to there' and it will move."

Oh that my faith could be this strong, this sure, this secure.

Genuine followers of Christ trust God and exercise active confidence in Him. They believe His Word and act on it no matter how they feel,

Faith Is the Foundation

because He promises a good result. When we exercise our faith, we have forward spiritual momentum. When we let our faith atrophy, we lose ground and fall away from Him.

No faith means no relationship with our Creator. As our faith increases, we begin an eternal relationship with Him.

Because faith forms our basic relationship with God, it is the foundational element of the Christian life. Love for others flows out of this faith relationship.

Faith is essential. Every good thing God wants to bring to our lives comes through faith. According to Hebrews 11:6, *it is impossible to please God without faith.*

That is the story of my walk, and I pray it is your story.

This walk is an act of faith. God clearly spoke to me. He wanted me to break the cycle of reliance on myself and learn to rely on Him.

Today I am stepping out in faith, trusting God will protect me from the elements, the cars, and the snakes. Yes, snakes. I've been told that the wildlife resource agencies catch rattlers and copperheads and release them along the trace. That is one of the reasons that I walk on the pavement as much as possible.

The choice of walking on the pavement or the soft shoulder was a consideration I weighed with God during my training. The downside of walking on the pavement is the heavy pounding on my feet, ankles, and knees and the proximity of traffic. The downsides of walking on the soft shoulder are snakes, chiggers, uneven terrain, and sinkholes. Listening to God led me to walk on the pavement as much as possible to avoid snake bites and the potential of twisted ankles from the rocks and holes that are hidden in the grass of the shoulders. Following God's direction in this aspect is an act of faith. Being more sure-footed allowed me to cover more territory daily.

I thought about the times I have intentionally relied on myself, not on God. I have not done what I committed to do all the time. There were times when I followed God's direction only when it suited me. I made excuses for why I didn't follow through with my promises to God, my family, and others.

My divorce from the mother of my children is one such blatant period when my self-interest and sinfulness caused me to ignore God. During that period, I made excuses for my sinfulness, blamed my wife, and even told friends that God had led me to the divorce. The surrender to the sin of self-centeredness caused me to worship myself rather than God. The sins of lust, self, and deceit caused me to break my promise before God that I would be faithful "till death do us part." In hindsight, I now see the pain my self-centeredness caused. I now understand Jesus's caution about divorce.

Sheryl's Notes

Today has been a little different for us. Just as we got in the vehicle lightning flashed through the sky like fireworks on the Fourth! Walking in a nice mist is wonderful but not in lightning and a downpour! We turned back into the parking lot, went straight to the room and crawled back into bed. The second time we got up this morning we ate again. By this time, we decided to pack up and head to our next destination, Kosciusko, Mississippi.

Early this afternoon, we arrived at our B and B, the Maple Terrace Inn, a beautiful two-story, Queen Anne-style brick home. Walking through the door is like going back in time. It was built in 1912 and was completely furnished with gorgeous antiques. The inn looks like a home you would imagine a rich, prominent politician would have lived in. I can visualize the old cars pulling up to the front waiting on the lady of the house to come out to go to church. It is currently owned by the local optometrist in town, who obviously has a love of antiques and preservation of old homes. B and B's give the traveler a little piece of calm away from home. They also give people a chance to learn more about the area and make new friends.

We are now back on the trace, and Troy is walking. The temperature is eighty-three and humid. It seems to get more difficult to get much distance toward the latter part of the week. Fatigue seems to build. He is resting a lot, and the "good wife" in me says he needs to eat and drink more.

The birds are not singing as much today, maybe due to the heat. I am at a pull-off about four miles from Troy. This is when I write and listen for God's whispers. This trip has really led me to realize how much I need to slow down. I am always so busy, never allowing myself the time to just be still.

Sheryl took me to MM 130 about 5:30 p.m., and I walked until 8:30—only eight miles tonight. Looking toward Friday and Saturday, I am ready for a good walking out in stronger faith.

Chapter 11

Disciplines of a Disciple

*If you can't fly, then run, If you can't run, then walk,
If you can't walk, then crawl, but whatever you do,
you have to keep moving forward.*
—Martin Luther King Jr.

July 11, 2014

LAST NIGHT SHERYL BEGAN SHOWING symptoms of an infection. When I arose about 4:30 a.m. and made the coffee, she said, "I feel a bit better. We should push on today." I made the coffee and sat on the porch to commune with Jesus. On my eleventh walking day, Sheryl drove us south to MM 137 at 5:50 a.m. even though she was not feeling well.

After a couple of easy days on the trace, my energy has returned. The weather is much cooler than I expected, and I am thanking God for it.

Today's Reflections

This urging from the Holy Spirit kept prodding me, *You must step up your Christian walk. The way you can love Me is to obey Me. Love Me by spending more time with Me.*

I began by examining how I am living my Christian life. Since I accepted Jesus as my Lord and Savior over sixty-five years ago, you'd think my life would be exemplary. While at times I feel I am the lowest of sinners, yet I am trying hard to live a better life.

As I've come to an understanding of the good news of the Gospel, I have found some disciplines for my Christian walk that help. From a human perspective, whether we are playing golf, growing a garden, financing a business, driving a vehicle, or grilling a steak, there are certain disciplines or rules to follow for success. I would like to say I have scored a perfect ten on each of these disciplines, but the truth is I have rarely come close to a ten on any one of them. But one of my core beliefs is the worth of life is found in reaching, though there are things we will never achieve.

The Bible encourages us to constantly grow toward sanctification. Just as a child grows and matures, so should a Christian. It is God's purpose that we become mature in Christ so that we eventually take on His image. It is against the law of nature and God for us to remain immature—mature human bodies but spiritual dwarfs. The apostle Peter writes in 2 Peter 3:18 that we are to grow. This implies steady maturation, constant development, and increasing wisdom so we can be productive and effective.

Ten Christian Disciplines

1. Be active in a church community.

As Christians we need to gather together to worship God. This discipline is the one in which I have performed the best. As a child in the Southern Baptist denomination, I attended church three times a week. After joining the navy at age seventeen, I maintained church attendance wherever I was stationed: San Diego to New London to Charleston, and many other ports in the Atlantic, Mediterranean, and Caribbean oceans.

Following the influence of my parents, worshiping regularly with other Christians has been a safe port for me—a place where I can repent for my sins of the week and receive forgiveness. Despite a few human flaws, church is the place where I experience God the most.

For the last dozen years, I have worshiped God in a small Methodist church in Leiper's Fork, Tennessee. Our congregation is composed of a wide variety of people from all age groups and church backgrounds. Generally, I have found the people of the church to be loving and supportive of each other. They have certainly shown me love and have helped me heal during the losses of divorce and my business.

2. Communicate with God, especially by listening.

Prayer has been my second strongest discipline. It is simply communicating with God, and a huge part of communication is listening. Listening to God has been an acquired practice for me. For many years my prayers consisted of asking God for my wish list followed by a quick amen. While I wasn't exactly ignoring God, it was as if His direction and requests of me were not relevant.

There have been long periods of my life when I had no designated prayer time except for prayers in church. There have been other stretches when my life was in turmoil that I prayed fervently. I have had the most joy during periods when I have prayed, listened, and meditated on God's Word.

My parents prayed for me and my protection. God answered their prayers even when I wasn't praying. My sister told me that after I left for the navy my parents prayed for me three times a day.

Once we had an accident on the submarine on which I served. We descended below our operating depth and then quickly several hundred feet below our test depth. The test depth is the depth to which the welded joints, the pressure hull, and connectors have been tested to be safe. Everyone aboard believed we were headed straight for a crushing death at the bottom of the ocean. After some terrifying minutes with many seals spewing seawater, we were able to right the angle of the submarine. After bringing the sub level, we were able to slowly surface. We all breathed great sighs of relief. I'm sure we had all prayed during those harrowing moments.

When I calculated the time difference, I realized this had occurred at exactly the same time my parents were praying back home for my safety.

Around the year 1990, I began allocating time during my prayers to listen in silence. I have lived these last twenty-four years with the same intense prayer cycle of regular and devoted prayer followed by periods of cursory communication with the Lord.

3. Ask for the Holy Spirit's guidance.

One of the most difficult aspects of the Christian walk has been to stand aside and let God take over all the choices and decisions of my life. But Romans 8 tells us the Holy Spirit prays for us. What a comfort that realization is to the weakest of us.

I was in a men's prayer group with a fellow who prayed for the most mundane things: for God to help him in a business meeting, digest his food, keep his allergies from flaring up, and heal his foot fungus, etc.

I thought, *Doesn't he have anything more significant to take to the Lord?* But he taught me a valuable lesson. God is interested in everything, and He will help us in all of it. My praying friend taught me to turn everything—even the things I think are trivial—over to Him.

Robin Brown, a friend of mine, shares her example of relying on God for everything in her life. She prays constantly for protection, for resources, and for things as mundane as a good parking space. Robin has an awesome testimony of her relationship with the Lord.

4. Be obedient to the Holy Spirit.

Not letting Christ have first place in all the choices of my life has been one of my greatest sins. I have ignored the Holy Spirit and have been self-centered and confident in my own ability. As I look back over my life, I can say all the big mistakes have been undertaken without prayer. I've made them on my own without consulting the Holy Spirit.

My walk on the trace is my way of being obedient to God's direction. The huge depression I felt over ending my career and selling my business is being healed by following the direction of the Holy Spirit. He is showing me I can find joy in my trials by going through more trials. Experiencing the feelings of worthlessness after selling my business was a trial. This walk is another difficult trial, but it is also causing me joy.

5. Study the Scriptures.

Until about five years ago, ninety-five percent of my Bible reading had been cursory speed reading to just get through it. But being involved with men's prayer groups and the Christian Leadership All-In program has taught and encouraged me to slow down and study Scripture, meditate on it, and pray for understanding and application. I am no longer content to skim through a chapter merely to satisfy my

Disciplines of a Disciple

conscience. Memorizing Scripture and hiding the Word in my heart has helped guide, correct, and encourage me. All we need is there.

6. Love God with your whole heart.

Jesus taught His followers this. Loving means spending time with Him. It means we desire to spend time with Him more than anything else. Oh, how I have failed in this command.

7. Love your neighbor as yourself.

As I review my life, I have experienced the most joy when I have served others. Jesus said, "By this shall all men know that ye are my disciples, if ye have love one to another" (John 13:35). The greatest demonstration that we are Christians is that we love one another.

8. Let the Holy Spirit fight life's temptations.

From an early age, I learned to depend on myself. I felt that I couldn't trust people. So I have led a life of yielding to temptation because I haven't enlisted the Holy Spirit to fight for me. Temptation is not sin. It is *yielding* that is sin. Let Christ through the Holy Spirit do the fighting for you.

9. Avoid pride and live humbly.

Being self-assured, selfish, and prideful has been the source of most of my sin. As a result, I have been humiliated many times in correction and discipline.

10. Avoid intentional sin, and be a wholesome Christian.

My intentional sinning still occurs, although at a much lesser pace than years ago. For years, I have annually reflected on this and gauged my growth on this discipline. I still intentionally sin but, thankfully, less.

Being a wholesome Christian attracts others to Jesus. I have had very little impact on the unsaved from trying to fit into their world rather than attracting them to mine. My daily life and appearance should commend the gospel and make it attractive to others.

Sheryl's Notes

This morning Troy brought my coffee up to the room. He always does this for me when we are traveling. He is so good to me! Troy had a thirteen-mile walk today. God is playing a huge part in this by giving us much cooler weather than we ever expected. Who has ever heard of seventy-five degrees with low humidity during July in Mississippi? (That was today!) It has to be pleasing to God to see Troy's faith expressed through his walk, so we know this is His way of taking care of us. This much-needed cooler weather was not a whisper from God; it was a shout!

Speaking of blessings, Community Care Fellowship received a huge blessing today! Lori and Lenny entertained the homeless while lunch was being served to almost two hundred people by Pastor Betty, Jonathan, Bruce, and Gavin. Can you imagine how this added sunshine to their lives? Our mission on this trip is to bring awareness to others regarding the homeless and to raise money for them. I hope to start going on a regular basis to serve.

It is 7:30 p.m., and Troy is still walking. I just don't know how he would have the strength without God's assistance. I feel this trip has brought us closer together. This is such a life-changing experience, and we are learning so much as we go.

Though I still felt I could continue, Sheryl picked me up at 10:30. I had covered thirteen miles and decided not to overdo. We went back to Kosciusko and took Sheryl to a doctor who prescribed an antibiotic for her infection. We then spent a little time that afternoon touring the city.

Kosciusko is a small town in Central Mississippi and home to about ten thousand people. We were surprised to learn this was the birthplace of Oprah Winfrey. As Oprah began her television career in Nashville, we always claimed her as a Tennessee native.

Kosciusko avoided strife during and after the Civil War. Citizens said they heard the cannons at a distance during that conflict, and once or twice soldiers rode through town, but never a shot was fired inside its city limits.

While Sheryl was in the doctor's office, I further reflected on the day. Possessing the personal discipline to carry out these ten actions is very difficult. Does this explain why so many people fall away from the Lord? As for me, I feel a deep joy when I have a day or week in which I have walked with God, doing my part.

Sheryl drove me back to MM 150 and waited at a rest area while I walked from 6:00 to 8:00 p.m., six more miles. The cooler weather was completely unexpected today. I was so very thankful for the cool breeze, fewer mosquitoes, and a total of nineteen miles today.

Chapter 12

Facing Trials

In the middle of the road of my life I awoke in a dark wood where the true way was wholly lost.
—Dante, Commedia

July 12, 2014

WHILE I HAVE RECEIVED CONFIRMATIONS that I should carry out this walk, today was the most magnificent confirmation I could have ever expected or predicted. God changed the weather. Was it just for me? Would it have happened if I had not carried out the walk? Was this climate change man-made or God-made?

After making my coffee this Saturday morning, I walked out on the porch for my quiet time with the Lord. I needed a jacket—it was chilly. I didn't bring a jacket, so I returned to the kitchen for my prayer time. The urging from the Holy Spirit was for me to reflect on the difficulties of life and how they have enabled me to grow as a person.

Just south of the Kosciusko exit, Sheryl dropped me off at MM 156. We both felt good this morning and were able to get an early start to enjoy the unseasonably cool weather. When I started, the temperature was fifty degrees. Walking in a thin cotton T-shirt, chill bumps ran all over my body, so I jogged for the first half mile or so to warm up.

Troy Waugh

Today's Reflections

The Holy Spirit directed me to focus on trials I've encountered along my life's journey. And He gave me a wonderfully crisp day to walk into the arms of Jesus. Is this God's way of telling me to "count it pure joy" when facing trials? Reflecting on trials in the midst of a glorious day helped me hold two opposing yet divine thoughts in my head at once and glimpse the divine opposites of which Jesus spoke.

Considering it all joy in the midst of trial is a sign of spiritual maturity, which I am slowly gaining. Early in my life, trials depressed me and left me asking, Why me? A few times I was very angry with God and everyone around me. In more recent years, I've learned to see hope and glimmers of joy. I can't always say it's pure joy. More often than not, I experience joy after some time has elapsed between the trial and the realization that I have learned something.

This walk is definitely a trial, yet I experienced incredible joy during training of the two previous months.

Mother's Trials

At my mother's funeral, I read James 1:2–4: "Consider it pure joy, my brothers and sisters whenever you face trials of many kinds, because you know that the testing of your faith produces perseverance. Let perseverance finish its work so that you may be mature and complete, not lacking anything."

I never knew the full story of the severe and unspeakable trials my mother endured during her lifetime. Anna Mae (Whitecotton) Waugh brought brutal emotional scars into her marriage and family. In the era in which she grew up, there was no one for her to talk with, no one who could help her face and resolve her traumas, and no one to prescribe Zoloft.

For all the years I remember, mother suffered regular bouts of deep suicidal depression. We never knew if the extreme depression she exhibited was caused by a chemical imbalance or from her childhood experiences. There were instances when she would become irate at the least little infraction. Once her brother made an unintended but hurtful remark, and she didn't speak to him for ten years afterward.

There wasn't a week when I wasn't slapped, spanked, beaten, or verbally scorned. In her most horrible moments, she would tell me,

"You are no good. Why did God give me you? You are ungrateful. I'm taking you to the reform school."

In her finest hours, she loved us by maintaining order at home and keeping us in clean clothes. Only in her final years was she able to utter the words I love you.

With my mother dealing with severe mental illness and my father absent much of the time, the abuse I dealt with caused me to be belligerent and angry—always ready for a fight. However, despite the ordeals I walked through, my parents were Christians, and they loved the Lord.

Both my mom and dad reached their twenties during the Great Depression. That experience was the source of much long-lasting fear for them. They witnessed the horrible events that took place when people went hungry, couldn't get jobs, abandoned their families, or committed suicide.

When my mother was thirteen, her mother died. As the eldest of six children, she was left to be the woman of the house. From 1924 through 1942, she devoted her life to her father, three brothers, and two sisters.

Rumors abounded in our family of many horrible events: my grandmother died hemorrhaging blood at home in front of her children and husband, my grandfather was a heavy drinker, and there was mental illness in her bloodline for which relatives were institutionalized. My grandfather treated my mother as his wife for years, and mother's siblings were very difficult and resentful toward her unskilled parenting. These rumors were never confirmed by my mother or her siblings but were spoken of in hushed tones reserved only for adults.

Dad's Challenges

My dad encountered difficulties in his life as well, but he didn't have to deal with the mental illness, abuse, and chaos of my mother's early years.

As one of seven children raised on a farm, he was used as farm labor and didn't graduate high school until he was twenty-one years old. He told me about the long days in the sweltering West Tennessee countryside, as he and his siblings worked the dirt, raised the hogs, cattle, and chickens, and survived totally off the land. With no electricity, no city water, and no telephone, the Waugh family faced daily trials they solved with optimism and hard work.

In 1934, at twenty-one years of age, Dad joined the US Army and served through World War II. He faced war in Germany and fought to defend our nation while putting his life at risk daily. Somehow he came through the trials of his life a total optimist.

Dad's positive approach had an overriding influence on our outlook on life, as most of the time both Alice and I tend to be optimistic. As he always, always, always saw the sunny side of the street, his optimism could sometimes border on the delusional. Had he been a pessimist, our lives would have been very dark. Alice and I marveled at the way Dad (who passed away at age sixty-four) kept such a positive attitude in the face of our mother's bouts of depression and his normal ninety-hour workweek. His positive attitude endured through business failures, the responsibilities of caring for a family, job loss, and his life-ending lung cancer.

My Young Life

Despite their challenging lives, my parents grew in their faith, which had the most influence on me. With my hyperactive mind, I struggled with why God allowed me to endure regular physical and emotional abuse. Then somehow, my challenges became normal. As a boy, I simply didn't let life get me down.

One Sunday night after church when I was six, my mother asked, "What curse word did you say in class?"

"I didn't say anything bad."

"Your teacher said you used a bad word. You need to tell me what it was!"

At first, I denied using any foul language. But when the whipping started, I began admitting to any curse word I knew in order for the whipping to stop.

I said, "Hell."

"No, that's not it," she said, and my father continued beating me with his belt.

"Damn," I yelled.

"No, that's not it. Tell me what you said."

I went through all the words I could muster. After each one the fresh belting began again. At that time, I only knew about six curse words. It felt as if the beating continued for hours.

To this day, I don't know if I ever said the right word or if they were just exhausted from whipping me. I was thrown out the back door of our house into the darkness. Battered, cold, scared, and alone, I crouched behind an old chest at the wall of the outside porch.

Where is God? I agonized. My parents didn't seem to love or care for me, so neither did God in heaven, I reasoned. Years later, I would write:

Alone and Scared

All alone and scared
My life force laid bare
Not sufficient, too small, too wild
Cage it in. Reject the child.
Contain that soul.
Only six, rejected, I felt abandoned, alone
Then I left one after the other so I could leave first.
I thought another girl would bring me home,
To feel secure, fulfilled, not alone.
Is this loneness really all the company I need?
We arrive alone and die alone.
Am I stronger than I believe?
Inside, the dry seeds blossom.
The gypsy wanders.
And I, who am no longer I,
Travel that winding stream
Crashing over rocks
Flowing over sand
Refreshing the deer
Rising to the sun
All alone and scared.

While I am sure I was a difficult child to handle, it seems the abuse meted out to me far exceeded my childish offenses. As I grew up, these over-the-top punishments helped me form coping mechanisms to navigate life. Mostly, they taught me the world is a harsh and unloving place and that family and relationships aren't to be trusted. They taught me to leave first, rather than be left. They informed my own parenting and marriage skills as I became an absent and harsh father and husband.

Everyone develops coping mechanisms from childhood wounds. While they are helpful for a child to survive, they are harmful when we become adults. When there is little love or guidance from parents, the coping strategies become huge habits and carry on into adulthood.

Growing Up

After being discharged from the navy, I enrolled at the University of Tennessee (UT) with a major in accounting. I was never a really great bean counter, so this didn't fit my personal profile. However, as a youngster walking to and from school, a CPA's office was in my path. Parked in front of his office building were three awesome Thunderbird convertibles: a 1955, a '56, and a '57. In my mind I conflated being a CPA with sports cars, so I chose to major in accounting. Thirty years later, I learned why God directed me in this roundabout career when I founded The Rainmaker Companies, consultants to the accounting industry.

During my sophomore year at UT, I met a beautiful brown-eyed girl one Sunday night at church. I told my college roommate later that night, "Tonight I met the girl I want to marry." About a year later, Carolyn Honeycutt and I were married, and we moved to Knoxville while I finished school. When our twins were stillborn, we were crushed. Our youthful hopes and dreams were dashed on the rocks of death.

I wasn't mature enough to carry the responsibility of marriage, and my level of woundedness led me into a life of infidelity, anger, quarrelsomeness, bitterness, deceitfulness, and greed.

Although I believed God had given me the gift of salvation through the sacrifice of His Son, I could not escape the sinful nature of my life even by trying as hard as I could. Sin led me into my first divorce, a self-inflicted trial that hurt my wife, hurt my two sons, and set me back in my Christian walk.

God promises to be with us in difficulties (Isa. 43:2–5). Even self-inflicted trials present a watershed moment in our lives. Satan sees God's children going through trials and takes advantage of our vulnerability and weaknesses. Sin that hasn't tempted one for a long time can overtake us during a trial when all our energy is directed toward surviving.

Rather than wallowing in my misery in trials, I should think, *I'm one of God's children, so I shouldn't be surprised by this trial. I should believe I would get through it with God's help.*

After we triumph through hellish times, the resulting sense of vitality and abundant life become a precious part of our memories. It's not the trial but our *response* to it that matters most. Though sin and temptation can be heightened in trials, suffering can also make us more focused in our walk with Christ.

Sometimes God gives us a new trial to place life in perspective, as me taking on this walk after retiring from business. I am in the midst of this "trial," walking 444 miles (plus nearly three hundred in training) and counting it as pure joy.

Wrapping up my week's walk at 10:30 on Saturday morning, July 12, I found I had covered 170 miles in two weeks (ninety miles this week). That is only seven miles short of my planned milestone for this portion of the walk. My feet, knees, and hips were extremely sore and the blisters on my heels were beginning to get larger. Taking off the rest of Saturday and all day on Sunday was certainly welcome.

Chapter 13

Life Is Hard

*Many owe the grandeur of their lives
to their tremendous difficulties.*
—Charles Spurgeon

July 14, 2014

AT BREAKFAST SUNDAY MORNING, WE met Peeler and Holly Lacey, the neatest couple from Laurel, Mississippi, visiting Kosciusko to attend Peeler's high school reunion. We enjoyed getting to know them over breakfast, and they invited us to First Baptist Church, just across the street from our B and B. After the service, we lunched together, then the Laceys gave us an insider's tour of the city. (Since then, we have traveled with them to Israel and attended an Ole Miss football game as their guests.)

Sunday evening, we moved north to French Camp, Mississippi, a small village adjacent to the trace, and will be staying in this location for a few days. French Camp, established in 1812 by Frenchman Louis Lefleur, was a trading post on the Old Natchez Trace. The French Camp Bed and Breakfast Inn is a quaint village of small cottages located about one hundred yards east of the trace. This will be the closest we've been able to sleep to the trace.

When we arrived, we felt like we'd found a beautiful jewel. Sheryl fell in love with French Camp. We stayed in the carriage house attached to our cottage, which housed Lefleur's carriage in a glass-enclosed garage. The welcoming chimes of the beautiful white Baptist church rang every hour.

Sheryl's Notes

French Camp Academy (FCA) was established in 1885 by Scotch-Irish Christians who established a boarding school for children. FCA has grown to accommodate 160 boarding students and provide families in the nearby communities with a quality Christ-centered education and atmosphere. The school is for students who need a more controlled atmosphere, often from single-parent families with troubled or abused children.

On the other side of the street is the quaint historic district, open to the public with little log cabins, a blacksmith shop, the inn, country store, etc. On our table in the carriage house where we are staying, there is a folder of poems written by the students. This one really touched my heart:

> My Daddy drinks his problems away.
> He drinks away his fears.
> Mommy says we must stay,
> And then bursts into tears.
>
> My Daddy drinks his life away.
> He drinks away his dreams.
> Mommy says "just one more day"
> And fills our hearts with screams.
>
> My Daddy drinks his hopes away.
> He drinks away my laughter.
> Mommy says we must go—
> To live happily ever after.

Can you imagine the pain in that child's life? There is no wonder many children today are confused and mixed up! It made me stop and wonder what some of the homeless have gone through as children. Are they escaping the pain of their upbringing? Were they severely abused?

Today's Reflections

I arose Monday morning full of energy and excitement for day thirteen. The Lord urged me to continue to think on the difficulties of life. Life is hard, and how we handle those hardships determines how we mature as people. The reflections of the last two weeks have been heavy. Many of these memories are buried in the trash pile of regret. While I don't believe I must walk constantly on my knees repenting, the despair I sometimes feel is overwhelming. I thank God for this time of a walking sabbatical across the beautiful landscape to remind me of His forgiveness and grace.

Although I am usually optimistic, occasionally I have become despondent over the losses and calamities of my life. My introduction to life was unpredictable, chaotic, and hard. It seemed as if I couldn't count on anyone and, as a result, grew self-confident and dependent only on myself. The large doses of stress, loss, disappointment, and fear I endured made me depend on myself more.

About thirty years ago I began changing my reliance to God when He challenged me to gain confidence in Him.

There have been two eight-year periods when I felt my hard times and discipline were for a purpose. One such period took place between 2002 and 2010 when I learned to pray about everything. The other eight-year period of discipline occurred between 1995 and 2003.

A Great Loss

I have come to realize the true value of family relationships after a great deal of grieving and soul searching. Having experienced the loss of relationship with a son, I have been able to relate to other men and women who've lost a child through estrangement or death. Let me tell you my intensely personal story of the joy that comes from trials.

My son Brian and I had enjoyed a beautiful, loving relationship all his life. Brian shared my mischievous streak, my sense of humor, and my hyperactive mind and body. He loves to introduce himself as "Troy 2.0." I must agree; he is the improved version. Brian has a tender heart of gold and regularly serves others. Excellent with his hands, he can build or repair most anything. Brian is a strong man, over six feet two inches tall, and 250 pounds—a gentle giant. Because of his tender heart, he shows his pain easily.

When Carolyn and I divorced, he began acting out in school and hanging with the wrong crowd of people to deal with the pain of the family breakup. Brian came to live with me because he felt I would be lonely. He needed his dad and also wanted to comfort me. During that period, we grew extremely close.

Brian has an amazing IQ and memory, but he struggled with testing in school. I invested extra time tutoring Brian, as well as hiring tutors to help him. Brian has been a dependable and steady worker and has earned an income since he was sixteen years old. In 1991, while he was attending college and drilling with the Tennessee Army National Guard, he started a part-time job as a truck loader with FedEx in Nashville.

A Crisis

Then our relationship fell apart.

The call came about 9:00 a.m. on a Friday from a doctor at Vanderbilt Psychiatric Hospital. He said, "Are you Brian Waugh's father?"

"Yes."

"Your son Brian has been admitted. We fear he is psychotic, may harm himself or others, and will need to be admitted to the state mental hospital."

I felt stunned and in disbelief. *How can this be true for my son?*

The doctor told me Brian had tried to hang himself, but fortunately the rope had broken. His roommate had called 911 as he heard the crashing furniture and Brian vomiting uncontrollably.

There were no words to describe the confusion, fear, and harsh self-blame I felt. Then a cold burning pain set into my soul. There hadn't been any clues that Brian was despondent or even depressed. I was about to learn that he had kept his downward spiral toward suicide to himself.

When I visited Brian at the Vanderbilt psych ward, he seemed hyper. (Fifteen years later, we learned this was the hypomania side of his bipolar disorder.) He was talking about getting himself in shape and wanted me to buy him some men's fitness magazines. The rope burns around his neck brought me to the brink of despair for him.

Over the next six weeks, Brian was allowed to leave the hospital, only to be readmitted twice more. Why was Brian so despondent that he would try to take his own life? Why couldn't he share his pain with me? Why hadn't I been more available to him? Why had I not initiated more contact?

During his ordeal, I learned a series of disasters had hit Brian all at once. He had been laid off from his job. He had maxed out his credit cards. He had flunked out of college, and his girlfriend had left him. All of this came crashing down on my beloved son, and it was too much for him to emotionally handle.

When something like this happens to your child, a parent goes into overdrive in an attempt to help. Sometimes in the helping, a parent's acts can be taken as unwelcome meddling by the child. That's what occurred with us. I quizzed Brian about how he felt about all his issues, and he seemed to be very candid with me.

After he described the breakup with the girlfriend, I called her. I asked her if the breakup was permanent and if there was any possibility of reconciliation. She told me the breakup was permanent and there was no possibility of reconciliation. I then asked her not to respond to Brian's requests to see her to allow the doctors to help Brian get through the sense of loss he was feeling. She agreed.

Within twenty-four hours, the girlfriend did go visit Brian in the hospital and told him that she had not come before because I had requested her not to. Brian felt betrayed and became angry with me. Over the next few weeks, I visited the girl and her parents together. During that visit, she again told us her relationship with Brian was over. However, within an hour of our visit, she had called Brian to tell him about my visit.

Communication Cut Off

Brian also deeply resented my second wife's influence over me. He felt her involvement in my parenting was to his detriment. He exploded in anger and told me, "I don't want to have anything to do with you ever again." He then cut off all communication with me.

During the following eight years, Brian would not respond to my communication attempts. I tried reaching him through a variety of letters, phone calls, and through other family members. Nothing I did worked.

As the months and years ground forward, there was a hole in the world that Brian held in my life. A center of affection and memory like no other was vacant.

This loss of relationship with my son is the most devastating difficulty I have endured. Any parent with children can relate to the horror of losing relationship with a child. There probably isn't any greater human love than the love for a son or daughter. Losing that relationship through an angry separation or death is almost unbearable.

During the eight years of relationship separation with Brian, I did a great deal of self-examination. I spent many hours with counselors and pastors and friends discussing my loss. I grieved when my parents died, but parents belong to our past. Brian was my future. Brian was my child in whom I had placed hopes and dreams for his good fortune and success. Brian, my son, was the boy I had loved with my whole heart.

Restoration

As the years passed, I deepened my prayer life and pleaded with God to restore our father-son love and relationship. Rev. L. H. Hardwick, my pastor, advised me to view my loss as a death. Those were harsh but realistic words of advice. Changing my perspective caused me to give up my manic attempts to restore the relationship myself and turn the situation over to God. Over time, I began to rely on God more and more and accept that He does things in His own time, not mine.

Today as I am writing this, the grief is not as intense as it was in the 1990s, but it has not disappeared. I still feel the emptiness in my heart and the futility of those awful days. When a friend shares a loss, I immediately return to those feelings. The pain of the loss rises to the surface of my soul, but also the memory of years of learning and ultimate redemption gladdens my heart.

Family relationships were down the list of importance for me. I took my marriage and my children too much for granted. So many other things distracted me—my pursuits in business, power, and money—that my anxieties and sorrows were kept tamped down. Brad and Brian are amazing gifts to me, and now one of those had been snatched away. I didn't know how much I truly loved him deep in my heart until he was gone.

When I awoke, Brian was on my mind; when I lay down to rest, fitfulness kept me alert. Whenever I saw a FedEx package or a FedEx truck, I thought of Brian and strained to see if he was delivering or driving. I longed to hear him laugh, feel his big arms around my shoulders.

Then a small present arrived. Just before Thanksgiving 1995, I came home, and my wife said, "Sit down, Troy, there's something you need to know." She told me Brian had fathered a child out of wedlock. The boy had been born about a month before on October 30, 1995. Within a few hours, I met my new little grandson, David. Of course, he fit the bill of being *grand*.

David has brought joy into my life where there had been despair from the loss of Brian. With his birth, my prayer life intensified regarding our relationship. I learned not to be so reactionary, to be more cautious about making decisions without much information, and to appreciate the gift of children more.

The men in my Monday morning prayer group prayed for me throughout the week and helped me grow spiritually and intensify my prayers for restored relationship. I began to develop deeper friends who were not just business contacts. Whenever I would run into one of the guys at church, at the movies, or at a restaurant, he would tell me, "I'm praying for you. I'm praying for Brian. We are going to get him back for you." Through regular prayer and communication, these men began to teach me about relationships and helped restore my faith in the Lord. We went deep in our friendships.

In the spring of 2001, a psychologist called and told me he had been working with Brian. He asked, "Would you be open to reconciliation?" Of course, I jumped at the chance.

Over the next few months, no more contact occurred. Then one day he called again and said Brian was prepared to meet and discuss our reconciliation. He said Brian had a great deal of anger toward me and would need to vent that anger. He advised, "You will need to stay calm and not respond in anger to Brian's need to vent."

After a few months, Brian and I met with his counselor and began the redemptive process of rebuilding our relationship and becoming father and son again. I lived the biblical story of the father and the prodigal son, and I was willing to do anything to restore my son to his rightful place in my world. I wanted to place a warm coat of love around him, put the family ring on his finger, and embrace him back into relationship.

Those weeks and months were not easy, but the restoration began. Thank God, after eight long years, the loss of relationship with Brian was restored. Today Brian and I have an amazing relationship. Brian has developed his own relationship with the Lord and has been blessed with a wonderful wife, Nicole. In April 2003, on one of the most amazing days of my life, I introduced my six-year-old grandson, David, to his father.

I have had to learn to intentionally celebrate God's goodness during the calamities and trials of life. My joy is renewed when I engage in this kind of grateful worship. In many cases, the joy came six months or a year later when I realized the lessons God provided. In recent years, as I continue to have faith that God is teaching an important lesson, I have learned to find joy during the trials. Having joy during trials is a sign of Christian maturity. The trials of hardship and heartbreak are preparing us for walking into our future.

I've learned that stress is the mental and emotional muscle-building training we need to grow and develop. Without stress, life would be nearly meaningless. Leaning into the painful feelings awakens us to how alive we are and how deeply we can feel.

We are never more malleable than when we are feeling defeated and in need of help, and we are reaching for a way out. As we grow through these unpleasant times, we come to understand we are stronger when a new opportunity walks into our lives.

In his book *The Grand Weaver*, Ravi Zacharias says, "If you do not believe that God is in control and has formed you for a purpose, then you will founder on the high seas of purposelessness, drowning in the currents and drifting further into nothingness."

"Eternal Father, Strong to Save" is a hymn written by William Whiting in 1860. The Anglican pastor grew up on the shores of England and was inspired by the dangers of the sea. This hymn is regularly called upon by ship's chaplains and sung during services aboard ships.

> Eternal Father, strong to save,
> Whose arm does bind the restless wave,
> Who bids the mighty ocean deep
> Its own appointed limits keep;
> O hear us when we cry to Thee
> For those in peril on the sea.

My prayer of thanksgiving rose to heaven as I neared the end of this wonderful day of reflecting on life's hardships. Thank you, Eternal Father, for leading me through the perils of life and the dangers or trials with joy and gratitude.

In two segments today, from 5:30 to 10:00 a.m. and again from 6:45 to 8:15 p.m., I had walked eighteen and a half miles. A pattern of a high level of energy seemed to propel me forward this week as well. The cool weather from the polar vortex and the flat parkway also contributed to me moving at a good clip.

Chapter 14

Healing Is a Journey

*Life isn't about waiting for the storm to pass,
it's about learning to dance in the rain.*
—Vivian Greene

July 15, 2014

WE SAVORED A GLORIOUS DAY and night at French Camp. The weather was spectacular beginning on Tuesday with early-morning temperatures in the low 50s. The terrain was relatively flat with beautiful farms on either side of the trace. Early-morning and late-afternoon shadows added depth and beauty to the tall silos, barns, and farmhouses. Corn and soybean fields showed signs of robust growth with the prospects of a bumper crop during harvest. Cattle, sheep, and horses seemed healthy and happy in their dining rooms of grasses. Thank you, Lord, for sixteen and a half miles this morning.

After a late morning rest, Sheryl and I ventured out on the land around French Camp.

Located ninety miles north of Jackson and eighty miles south of Tupelo, the town and school together form a thriving nine-hundred-acre community.

Troy Waugh

Sheryl's Notes

Due to the drop in humidity and temps, Troy is able to walk longer. His goal is twenty-four miles today, and he is feeling great. In taking advantage of this nice weather, he wants to walk as much in a day as he can physically stand.

This is such a nice community, almost like going back in time. The population is about 160 people, not including the students. Today as we were walking in the area, the bells of the little Baptist church in the heart of town were playing.

If possible, I would really enjoy making this my mission—to bring these bells to our church's bell tower. Every day at noon and at 6:00 p.m., hymns play for ten to fifteen minutes. It is such a wonderful sound, reminding everyone of our Lord.

Well, tomorrow we will be leaving this sweet little community and heading north. God is blessing us richly on this trip. We will hit the halfway mark tomorrow—222 miles!

Today's Reflections

Learning more about the French Camp mission for wayward boys and girls inspired me to think about the journey of healing today. We all have hurts and pain we carry with us every day. God not only knows and cares about all our hurts, He wants to heal us and help us live more successful lives. The primary purpose of Jesus's ministry was to heal and redeem lost and hurting humanity.

Compared to many other people, my difficulties have been small. But to me, they are huge milestones of growth. Thank God, I haven't had to face dealing personally with serious mental illness, incurable disease, or a horrible accident. However, for decades I certainly repressed my woundedness.

The lyrics to Bill Gaither's song "Because He Lives" come to mind: "God sent His Son; they called Him Jesus; He came to love, heal, and forgive."

I have carried this poem by John Greenleaf Whittier in my notebook for years:

Don't Quit

When things go wrong, as they sometimes will,
When the road you're trudging seems all up hill,
When the funds are low and the debts are high,
And you want to smile, but you have to sigh,
When care is pressing you down a bit,
Rest, if you must—but don't you quit . . .

Success is failure turned inside out—
The silver tint of the clouds of doubt—
And you never can tell how close you are,
It may be near when it seems afar;
So stick to the fight when you're hardest hit—
It's when things seem worst that you must not quit.

For Sam Howard, French Camp offered a chance to escape his troubled home life and live in a home where he could benefit from structure and loving discipline. When he was two years old, Sam's father left the family. With his mother struggling with drugs, Sam was sent to French Camp, his first experience with what a real home life should be.

After a few years, Sam had the opportunity to resume life in his mother's home. Although he was happy to be with her, before he was even thirteen years old, his life quickly deteriorated into parties, drinking, and skipping school. He was sent back to French Camp. This time he was old enough to realize the loving discipline provided by his house parents, Randy and Joy Martin, was what he needed to get his life back on the right path.

Sam says he decided to do his best and turn his life around. "Sam was grateful to be here," says Randy Martin. "He would talk to the other kids and help them with their problems. He really became a leader in his time here."

Randy and Joy Martin were planning on becoming missionaries. After college they wanted to get jobs first to pay off student loans before serving in a ministry. "Little did we know when we got to French Camp that our long-term opportunity for ministry was right here," says Randy. "I get to use my degree in pastoral counseling every day."

Many students who come to French Camp come from home situations that are less than ideal. "We usually see an improvement in behavior in just a few weeks," Martin says, "but what we are really seeking is a heart change. We want these kids to feel loved and accepted. We want them to know that all the structure and routine is for their benefit."

My Own Healing

For many years I lived in denial that I had ever been wounded. This began at the time I told my father after a whipping, "That didn't hurt." Through much of my adult life, I put up a shield or mask that said, You can't hurt me; I won't allow it.

Mental wounds acquired during childhood sink into the unconscious and cannot heal on their own. Jesus asked a man, "Do you want to get well?" Healing isn't simply a one-time act of God, but a partnership between God and us. If we want to get well, we must do our part.

To begin healing, I had to work to understand the underlying wound. It is not sufficient to know how to behave properly. Knowledge and real comprehension are two different things. A skilled counselor asked me questions that made me probe into my psyche and begin to see the places that needed healing.

I had to stop making excuses for my behavior and take responsibility for my anger. Often we don't experience the breakthrough God has for us because we aren't willing to be obedient and responsible. We don't like change because it means we have to live differently.

We must be alert to recognize the patterns of behavior that are rooted in internal woundedness and what triggers outbursts, and we must shoulder the responsibility for that behavior. When negative emotions such as sadness, jealousy, unhappiness, or anger appear, instead of turning our attention to the environment for a reason, we must concentrate on the specific emotion itself.

If I feel anger, I'll do my best to experience it completely. Speak to it, name it, and tell it that it has protected me all these years, but now I am adult enough to handle these situations. Then I try to return to the past to find the root core of the anger, the original internal wound that fuels that particular emotion. The feelings that erupt from examining that wound are often frightening.

Finally, healing isn't focused on just relieving our pain or problems. It is focused on redeeming God's eternal purpose for our lives. It is possible for emotional and psychological traumas to be healed. God wants to use my scars and pain to help other people. After working over many months with a licensed Christian counselor, my wounds have been salved and the destructive anger modified.

With my morning and evening walks combined, I ended the day at MM 212 about 8:30 p.m. I had moved 23.5 miles today! It's the most mileage I've achieved in one day! Thank you, Lord.

Chapter 15

Dealing with Rejection

Rejection is like exercise; people say it's good for you, you know they're right, but it can be still tough to swallow.
—Author Unknown

July 16, 2014

I HAD THE COFFEE PERKING about 4:30. Sheryl reminded me it was my job to make the coffee—she said, "It's in the Bible—He brews." The predawn hour with my cup of hot coffee is the perfect time to visit with the Lord. The first fruits of my day. The first thoughts of the day. The first to-do of the day that might change all the other to-dos on the list.

After driving us past the little towns of Jeff Busby, Ballard Creek, and Pigeon Roost, Sheryl dropped me off at 5:30 a.m. About 8:30, my stepdaughter, Leanna McCaleb, along with Daniel Hunt (the only child of Leanna's fiancé, Jason), surprised me to walk across and celebrate my halfway mark.

Leanna is Sheryl's daughter. Although Leanna struggled with dyslexia, and teachers told her she wouldn't succeed, she has earned her bachelor's and master's degrees and is a high school biology teacher and coach. An amazing woman, she is highly intelligent, applies her gifts as a triathlete and a youth director, and is an inspiration to us all. When she learned about my plans to walk, she developed a personal training regimen for me and invested many hours coaching me on the proper shoes, socks, blister avoidance and care, nutrition, hydration, and endurance training.

During my brisk morning stroll up the trace, the weather was glorious for July—cool temperatures, a pale blue sky, and a soft breeze that plucked at my shirt sleeves. Today will bring celebration as I reach the halfway mark at MM 222.

Today's Reflections

Having prayed and reflected on trials, hardships, and healing, today seemed to be the time to reflect on the root of many of those trials—the feelings of rejection, fear of rejection, not feeling loved, needed, or cared for.

Fear immobilizes some people. Fear is caused by potential loss. People fear being turned down, losing good health, looking foolish, or losing money or status. Some fear spiders, snakes, the dark, losing those they love, or losing their lives. Perhaps more than anything else, we fear losing acceptance from others. Fear of rejection is widespread. In tribal times, being ousted from the safety of a group could have meant death. No wonder many of us try to fit in.

Initiating anything requires an element of risk. To laugh is to risk appearing foolish. To cry is to risk appearing sentimental. To love another is to risk rejection. To expose feelings is to risk revealing our true selves. To suggest creative new ideas is to risk ridicule. To try is to risk failure. But the greatest hazard in life is to risk nothing at all. Risk must be taken. Many people fear the outcome of a risk taken and settle for the sad life that "no risk" produces.

A certain amount of fear keeps us alert and safe—like a speed limit sign or a police car. But too much fear can immobilize us and can cause the loss of the very thing we feared losing.

Fear of Rejection

William is a friend of mine whose fear of rejection has nearly ruled his entire life. Because of his reluctance to fully engage with others, fear has damaged his relationships. "I felt like I was always the outsider, trying desperately to be accepted, to fit in. As my father was in the navy, we moved around the world many times while I was growing up. I went to six different schools in twelve years, each time trying to break into the in crowd. After a few attempts, I just accepted my rejection and began hanging out with the other outcasts. I vividly recall craving acceptance and losing my willingness to reach out for it!"

Whenever William is introduced to a new person, his neck and face flush red. He's quit school, relationships, and jobs without having another one lined up. Because of his intentional abandonment of friendships at the slightest hint of rejection, William has experienced the loss of many friends and girlfriends. He said, "To protect myself, I left them before they left me. It gave me a belief that I could be the rejecter and save myself from the pain of being rejected." He added, "I even look for signs that my wife or my children may reject me."

While I relate closely to William, I have been too proud to openly seek reassurance. He, on the other hand, is continuously asking, "Are we okay? Are you mad at me? Are you really my friend?" William said a group of his friends went to the movie one night and didn't invite him. He felt overwhelming rejection.

William does not like his present job, but because of the fear of rejection, he will not seek new employment. He is unable to send his resume, make a phone call, or knock on a door. He has allowed himself to thwart his own growth potential from the fear of rejection.

William told me when he believes a group will reject him, he begins feeling anger with the group. People in the group sense his anger and reject him. Then he believes he was right from the very beginning: "I told you so! I *knew* it!" William wants to be proved right—even if it means a bad outcome. Expecting and receiving the bad outcome almost acts as a type of emotional insurance policy.

A hypersensitivity to the signs of rejection can make us needy, clinging, and subservient, allowing *any* action, look, or word from others to be interpreted as a pending rejection, when it simply isn't.

FEAR—False Evidence Appearing Real

I once heard Zig Ziglar say fear is "false evidence appearing real." Fear of rejection is often a self-fulfilling prophecy that makes us act in a way that the false idea comes true. If you wrongly believe you will lose a game, you may become protective, conservative, quiet, even angry. When I shut down, my change in personality brings about the feared rejection that wasn't there to begin with.

I can even feel it in my golf game. While my game is not up to that of a scratch golfer, I have the skill to break ninety consistently. However, when I begin to fear my golf partner will think less of me if I hit a bad shot, I become anxious and conservative. That bit of tension creates the environment to top the ball or to miss a hit.

Franklin Roosevelt famously said, "There is nothing to fear but fear itself." FDR believed fear could immobilize a nation and could be a self-fulfilling prophecy. We see it all the time when people fear the worst from a new law, a new adventure, or a new opportunity.

A great baseball player is a good example. One who hits .350 is considered to be one of the best who ever played the game. A .350 hitter strikes out sixty percent of the time. But to get a hit, the batter often swings the bat two or three times. He also refuses to swing at many balls. He misses over ninety-five percent (either a strike or a ball) of his chances to hit a ball.

Acceptance of the misses is necessary in dealing with the fear of rejection. At Rainmaker Academy, we helped CPAs learn to sell their services. The most difficult aspect was to get them to pick up the phone, send an email, or ask for an appointment. The CPAs didn't want to feel rejected. We helped them decide how they *did* want to feel. Once the CPA understood the numbers game, he or she could be very successful. Once they committed to the ten phone calls and had success setting appointments and getting new business, many of them overcame that fear. From that point forward, they were able to see positive results and not let unrealistic fear slow them down.

Praying for a positive outcome, accepting a few missteps, and moving forward as if we own the outcome will completely change our results. Allowing myself to be led by the Holy Spirit has been key for me in overcoming my human fear of rejection. In a task that involves risk or an action where I sense I could fail or be rejected, I place my faith in God above all else. This gives me the courage I need to move forward. That is why it is crucial to pray and listen for what God wants for us. Only then are we able to break the cycle of fear.

When I bring God into my planning and listen to the counsel of the Holy Spirit, I gain enormous confidence in moving into a task that I might otherwise forgo. Praying with more confidence means being *less* sure you know what is going to happen. Then I can relax and be confident the Holy Spirit will bring me good things. Relaxing into the arms of Jesus and accepting any outcome has been the key for me to enjoy life.

If I discover a valuable antique, but through ignorance or shortsightedness believe it to be worthless junk, what does this say about me?

That reminds me of the story of a man who told his friend he had trashed an old family Bible that had been printed by "Guten something."

His friend said, "Gutenberg? He was the inventor of the printing press. Do you realize that Bible could have been worth nearly $400,000?"

"I'm sure it couldn't have been worth that much . . . the name of some guy called Martin Luther had been scribbled all over it."

Many musicians were rejected numerous times before achieving stardom. Many great authors were rejected before hitting it big. Great art is often rejected in the artist's lifetime.

When I am rejected, I cannot allow myself to feel it's because I'm unlovable. It just may have something to do with the other person.

I thanked the Lord today for sending Leanna and Daniel to accept and embrace me . . . and for building my identity in Him so the sting of human rejection is lighter.

Sheryl walked with us as we reached halfway at MM 222 and took some joyful photographs. We walked another three miles to wrap up the morning at 9:30 with thirteen miles (another half-marathon) behind us. Sheryl, Daniel, Leanna, and I enjoyed some chocolate milk and lunch and hung out together for a while before Leanna and Daniel returned home to Centerville. What a glorious day. Thank you, God, for family, for health, for great weather, and for confidence to complete this journey walking with You.

Chapter 16

The Power of God

Some morning, get up and allow the power of God to come on you, and allow Him to bless you.
—A. W. Tozer

July 17, 2014

WE HAVE HAD EXTRAORDINARILY MILD weather. I've felt strong and pushed to do fifty-five miles in three days. This morning I am feeling the effects of pushing hard. The fatigue was overwhelming, so I rested much of the day. I am finding it challenging to predict how far or how fast I can travel each day and how one day might affect the next.

After resting most of the day, soaking my feet and ankles, I had renewed energy. With the weather so cool and the humidity low, I wanted to push on.

My heel blisters had grown to the size of silver dollars and hurt for the first mile or so. Then my feet seemed to go numb. I consider it another wonderful gift from God when He takes my pain away. Leanna has coached me on soaking my feet and ankles in ice water to reduce the inflammation. Using a salve called Monkey Butt and heavy padding over the blisters reduced the expansion of the blisters and chances of infection.

After resting most of the day, Sheryl took me to MM 225 in the

Tombigbee National Forest around 5:30. By 8:20, at a much slower pace than normal, I had covered only nine miles. It was frustrating that with the beautiful, unseasonable weather I was unable to keep my usual pace.

Russ Corley called three times. He sensed the elation bubble I felt passing the halfway mark yesterday had burst, and he was right. His encouragement and friendship are extremely motivating, and he helped me move through the pain and fatigue in the afternoon.

I enjoyed having time to think, pray, and rest today. The welcomed cooler weather was so very unexpected. The TV weatherman mentioned Mississippi was experiencing a Canadian air mass. God seemed to be saying to me, *You followed my directions for this walk, and I am changing the weather just for you.* Was I hallucinating, or was God talking to me? Would He change the weather pattern in the entire state just for me?

Today's Reflections

As my body was weakening, the Lord whispered, *Focus on My power rather than yours.*

I wondered, *Will my personal encounter with God and His direction for me to carry out this walk be misunderstood?* Would it seem presumptuous to attribute specific directives or events to God? I believed I was being obedient to His direction to walk the 444 miles of the Natchez Trace in July 2014 and to finish on my seventieth birthday. Raising money and awareness for Community Care Fellowship was also God's instruction to me.

Understanding the mind and power of God is impossible for any human. We can only capture tiny glimpses. We must trust in the infinite and eternal power of God our Creator. Someday we will learn everything about God, but for today, I accept what is given for me to see. I know God created the universe, all things big and small.

Although the sun is ninety million miles away, we can feel its direct effect. When I walk from the direct sunlight into the shade of a building, the temperature drops several perceptible degrees. How can we ever understand the power of the sun? Scientists have estimated that the gravitational attraction of the sun's core produces temperatures that can reach more than twenty-seven million degrees Fahrenheit. Can you imagine a huge ball of fire that never burns itself up? God created that.

Consider the vastness of the universe. Have you ever looked up

The Power of God

into the night sky and wondered just how many stars there are in space? Look into the sky on a clear night when you are out of the glare of streetlights, and you will see a few thousand individual stars. With even a modest amateur telescope, millions more will come into view. Scientists and astronomers understand less than one percent of the universe.

Stars are not scattered randomly through space; they are gathered together into vast groups known as galaxies. The sun belongs to a galaxy called the Milky Way. Astronomers estimate there are about one hundred thousand million stars in the Milky Way alone, with millions upon millions of other galaxies besides! God created all that.

The vastness of the universe is one thing, but God also created the smallest, most intricate organisms and life forms.

George Washington Carver is said to have prayed, "God, help me to understand your mind." And God answered, "George, that's a little too much for you to handle, let's try a peanut." Carver found untold uses for the peanut and for many other agricultural products.

We grapple with trying to understanding the human body, what makes it tick, what makes it sick, what makes it strong, and how to affect it. We invest extraordinary amounts of money on research to cure diseases and yet many of the treatments we receive are educated guesses. God created the human body.

High Water and Dry Books

In May 2010, when Middle Tennessee experienced a five-hundred-year flood, many homes, businesses, museums, concert venues, and parks were destroyed or damaged. Though it was predicted that rain would move on through the area, when the front arrived in Nashville, it stalled for three days.

Several months before the big flood, my son Brian and I visited Sweetwater House in Accra, Ghana, along with Steve French. For years we had supported the ministry established by Steve and Debbie French and several others. Sweetwater House provided safe twenty-four seven lodging for two years for young women between the ages of fourteen and twenty-two, many of whom had been bought out of slavery. There were twenty-four young women residents along with eight interns (former residents who had graduated from the two-year program) and several adult teachers and counselors. The girls were provided with education, Christian counseling, classes, meals, clothing, medical care, and occupational training to sustain themselves after graduation.

Brian and I worked on the facility, met all the young women, and cooked and served them a meal one day before we left.

We noticed the bookshelves in the library were almost empty. On our flight home, God placed on our hearts to gather books and ship them to Sweetwater House. Shortly after Brian and I returned, we spread the word that we were gathering books suitable for teenage girls to be shipped to the orphanage in Ghana. Our friends were very generous, and we shipped hundreds of books.

A few days before the May 2010 flood, I had gathered six cardboard boxes of books to be shipped to Sweetwater. I unloaded the books and set them on the floor of my garage, not expecting the flood to be on its way toward us. We lived on a road with a huge ridge directly behind our house. Our detached garage sat about fifteen feet from the house with its floor about ten feet below that of the house.

On Sunday morning the rain had been pouring for about thirty-six hours. Sheryl and I sat on the front porch and watched flood waters pour down the road and completely immerse the four-foot-tall fence. About 10:00 a.m., I could see water pouring down the hill and driveway into the access door of the garage. When I entered the garage, the water covered the concrete floor about four to six inches deep. The closed garage doors on the other side were slowing the water from draining.

I had forgotten about those six boxes of books sitting on the concrete floor beside the Tahoe. But the books were untouched. There was water all around but no water had reached them, and the concrete around them was completely dry. I opened the tailgate and lifted the books into the back of the truck. Within a few minutes of moving the boxes, the water flooded over the dry area. The only explanation for this event is that God protected the books bound for Sweetwater House.

After the flood waters receded, I inspected the garage and the floor. The watermark was about four to six inches up the walls. I used a level and placed it all around the area where the books had been sitting and the garage floor was at the same level throughout. What an amazing miracle!

Back in May, Sheryl and many others warned me, "Don't do this walk in July. Wait until October when the weather is cooler." But I felt sure God's instruction was July, not October. Today I am beginning to understand that God knew something about the weather that no one else did—that July 2014 would be the coolest July on record in Mississippi.

In early July 2014, NBC news predicted a "cool wave sweeping away summer's heat. Morning temperatures could dip into the 50s for many next week, potentially setting seasonal records." It was extremely rare, although not unheard of, for a cold front to sweep that far south in July, bringing relief from humidity even for a few days at this time of year. Yet that is what happened.

Over the last fifteen or twenty years, there has been a great deal of controversy surrounding global warming and climate change. Some advocates believe man is responsible for the warming of the planet, while others seem to believe it is only changed by God.

Temperatures on earth have increased approximately 1.8 degrees Fahrenheit since the early twentieth century. Over this time, atmospheric levels of greenhouse gases such as carbon dioxide and methane have increased. Both sides in the debate surrounding global climate change agree on these points. I am not a man-made-global-warming believer, as it seems that none of the predictions of the alarmists have panned out. The change advocates like to say the science is settled. Science is never settled. And it seems there is a huge profit motive behind the climate change alarmists.

The pro side argues rising levels of atmospheric greenhouse gases are a direct result of human activities such as burning fossil fuels and that these increases are causing significant and increasingly severe climate changes including global warming, loss of sea ice, sea level rise, stronger storms, and more droughts. They use harsh tactics to shut down conversation and debate. They name call. They besmirch the motives of people who don't agree with them in a crude attempt to delegitimize debate. Because their tactics are so strident, I tend to lean the opposite way.

The con side argues human-generated greenhouse gas emissions are too small to substantially change the earth's climate and that the planet is capable of absorbing those increases. They contend that warming over the twentieth century resulted primarily from natural processes such as fluctuations in the sun's heat and ocean currents.

My belief is simple: God instructed me to walk in July, and He is now rewarding me for my obedience. That's my story and I'm sticking to it!

Sheryl's Notes

This weather has been a gift from God for Troy and his walk. I am so proud of him and admire his determination in finishing this journey when it would be so easy to quit. Troy has had days with quite a bit of pain from his tight muscles, knees, and just aching all over, but he will not give up! As a dedicated Christian, He wants to obey God's calling. That is just the man he is.

He hit the halfway mark! We were surprised and thrilled Leanna and Daniel came to join us in the walk. It really means a lot to have family and friends' support. Leanna has been Troy's coach in teaching him how important his nutrition and fluids are during this time. David Keedy, who was a Navy SEAL, also helped us as he knows all about this type of body stress.

We are in Tupelo now at a hotel. I am grateful for having a place to lay my head, food to eat, and hot coffee in the mornings, unlike the homeless. Speaking of the homeless, I talked with the man cleaning our room today, who told me about a tent city in Tupelo. Many of the townsfolk did not like it, so they have pressured the homeless to move out from this area, but they really do not have a place to go. He was excited about us being on this journey. Hopefully our conversation will give him the encouragement to reach out to the ones who cannot help themselves in the Tupelo area. We are touching lives one person at a time!

Today we visited Elvis Presley's home. It was really touching to go back in time and visit the actual little church he attended and see his very simple two-room home that is smaller than the size of our hotel room. Elvis did his first radio broadcast at ten years old. They attribute much of his love for music to the hymns he listened to in church as a child. He loved his gospel music! God certainly blessed him with talent. The Beatles were my favorites, but Elvis was my sister's!

About 5:30 p.m., I mustered up the strength to get back to MM 225. But I walked only nine miles in three hours, a miserable pace, but nine miles nonetheless. Maybe tomorrow morning I will be energized and can move better.

Chapter 17

Hearing the Voice of God

God did not stop speaking when the Bible went to press.

July 18, 2014

FRIDAY MORNING WAS OVERCAST AND damp. My quiet time with the Lord was inspiring. I prayed, "Lord, feed me today with your blue mist covering the summer fields and the fragrance of freshly mown grass. Help me hear your voice."

At 5:30 a.m., Sheryl dropped me off at MM 234, a little south of Tupelo. We had talked about going home for two nights so I could recover from my exhaustion. Around 6:30 a.m., traffic on the trace began to pick up considerably and the clouds began to sprinkle. Having to stay on the steep slopes of the shoulder today made walking extremely difficult and dangerous. I inched my way north toward Tupelo with morning rush-hour traffic shifting into high gear.

About 7:30, the clouds opened up and cold rain began to pour. So around 8:00, with only seven miles under my belt, I had to call Sheryl to come get me. She drove south and picked me up at mile marker 241, and we agreed to throw in the towel for the week.

I was physically spent. This was quite a contrast from Monday when I experienced the highest level of energy I've felt. I have given it everything my body can stand this week.

We checked out of our hotel and drove the 200 miles to our home in Leiper's Fork. There I spent the weekend nursing my feet and legs and sleeping. Sheryl and I enjoyed two days and nights at home.

It was especially good to attend our close-knit church and see our friends.

Tharina DaBeer saw me walking stiff legged and suggested I start getting into a pool of cold water. Tharina is a keen observer of a person's physical needs and has trained world-class soccer players in her home country of South Africa. As the soreness in my hips, knees, and ankles worsened by the day, her advice was crucial to my completing the walk. For the remainder of my walk, I stepped into a pool several times a day and sat in tubs of cold ice water to calm aching muscles and joints. Thank you, Tharina. Isn't it amazing how God is placing so many knowledgeable and wonderful people in my path?

Sheryl's Notes

> Just off the trace in Collinwood, we met the nicest young man (about twenty-five) from Seattle. It was raining, and he had stopped at a welcome center to shower and rest. He had ridden his bike all the way from Seattle and is heading to New Orleans! He is camping along the way. This makes our trip look like a piece of cake!

Today's Reflections

Today while walking, I focused on listening to the voice of God, the urging of the Holy Spirit, and meditating on the loving care of Jesus. While I have felt the urging of the Holy Spirit many times, I believe I have heard the audible voice of God twice. The audible voice of God was clear, unmistakable, strong, and definite. On the other hand, the Holy Spirit's urgings and nudgings seem more subtle.

Have you ever heard God speak to you? Have you felt strongly convicted through prayer to move in one direction or another? Has anyone ever given you a word spoken from the Lord? Have you been reading Scripture and received a strong urging to do something related to your reading?

There's a saying: "When you talk to God, it's prayer, but when God talks to you, it's schizophrenia." But hearing a voice when alone, or seeing something no one else can see, is pretty common. At least one in ten people say they've had such an experience. About four in ten say they have unusual perceptual experiences between sleep and awareness.

Part of me is afraid to listen to God as He may instruct me to do something I don't want to do. I'll have to admit, when I've put together plans for a business decision or a vacation, a small part of me resists when someone says, "Let's pray about this." God might want me to do something else. Even though my experiences of not listening to Him have caused me grief, there is still some part of me that feels asking God may result in a disruption to my plans. I am slowly learning that asking God is an act of holiness, an act of living by faith, and choosing to walk with my Creator and Friend.

Many Christians believe God speaks to them in various ways. The difficult part is determining whether it is God who is speaking or the spicy burrito we had for dinner. I had always thought God would speak to me when I was praying, calling on His name, or worshiping Him. Both times when God spoke to me, I was doing something else. God doesn't speak when I am ready—He speaks when He is ready.

From Scripture, we see God spoke when He was ready to speak to Moses, Samuel, David, and Paul. Though I certainly don't place myself in the category of these spiritual giants, I do believe God cares about the smallest of details and the smallest of people, even li'l ole me.

Hearing God's Voice

It was one morning in April 1991 when God spoke audibly to me for the very first time. I heard a clear, strong voice coming through my eardrums. I had no doubt it was God. The words were in English and had an absolutely self-authenticating ring of truth. I know beyond the shadow of a doubt that God didn't stop speaking when the Holy Bible went to press. He is God.

It happened as I had left my office in downtown Nashville to grab an early lunch. God said, "*I want you to go back into the accounting profession where you started and become a consultant to that industry. I have prepared you all your life for the challenge of starting up a new venture from scratch."*

There was not the slightest doubt in my mind that those were the very words of God. God spoke to me with absolute authority. I sat down on a bench and paused to let this sink in. God was near. He had me in his sights. He had something to say to me.

I felt enveloped in the love of God. The God of the universe was speaking to me. I wondered what He meant by "a consultant to that industry." How had He prepared me? A wonderful reverence settled over me, and I felt a palpable peace. This was a holy moment and a holy corner of the world in downtown Nashville, Tennessee. God Almighty was present and speaking to me.

Then He said, as clearly as any words have ever come into my mind, *"There was a purpose in the many start-up situations you have experienced."*

My heart leaped up, "Yes, Lord! You are awesome. Yes, I will do what you ask."

That these words were spoken out loud and penetrated my ear was breathtaking. I was stunned and just soaked in the glory of God. I heard the words of God as clearly as if at this moment my son was saying, "Dad, I'm hungry."

During the previous two years, I had experienced a renewal of my faith. I was investing in quiet time daily, talking to God, and trying to listen for His voice, His urgings, and His direction. But on that day, I was imbued with a fresh sense of God's reality.

I've learned that God speaks to His people in several ways:

Through Conviction

In John 16:8, Jesus said the Holy Spirit would come and would "convict the world concerning sin and righteousness and judgment." I think every Christian who is open to the urgings of the Holy Spirit experiences this gentle conviction.

This has been mostly my personal experience in hearing God. It's like a tapping on my shoulder, a whispering in my ear, or an urging deep inside me. There have been many times in my life when I have been convicted of my sinful nature. God has revealed to me the sins of pride, greed, lust, and deceit. When convicted, I began working to be more obedient to His Word.

Other times I have been convicted that I have not loved God with my whole heart or my neighbor as myself. He has pointed out to me that most of my sins were selfish in nature—concerned about me and my wants and desires.

Through Scripture

Many people report God speaking to them through the Scripture. I have often felt strong revelation and urgings from God-inspired Scripture. It is truth for our day as well as the time in which it was written.

Unfortunately, experiences in this world have taught us to believe lies. For example, I learned very early in life to protect myself by building a false image of myself. Because I believed I wasn't loved, I acted very independently and brashly with people and never asked for help.

But from the Scriptures, I have learned I am a son of God, an heir to His kingdom, and have been chosen to experience eternal life. We know God is the author of Scripture through the Holy Spirit (2 Peter 1:21).

If you feel you have been convicted of something, but it doesn't match scriptural principles, then you can be sure God did not reveal it. We've all heard falsehoods: "God wanted me to divorce." "God wanted me to lie so as not to hurt her feelings." "God wanted me to have this, so I'll just take it."

God speaks to the twenty-first century today through the Bible with greater force, greater assurance, and greater guidance than can be heard through any human voice. The Bible is the very voice of God. The great need of our time is to experience the living reality of God by hearing His Word personally.

Audibly

I have heard God speak audibly to me twice, in April 1991 and in April 2014. He may have spoken at other times, and I missed it.

God the Father spoke audibly to Jesus for others to hear when He was baptized. "A bright cloud overshadowed them, and a voice from the cloud said, 'This is my Son, whom I love; with him I am well pleased; listen to him!'" (Matt. 17:5). God spoke to Paul out loud on the road to Damascus. God can and does speak audibly today. He did not stop speaking when the Bible was written.

Visually

I've read reports of Jesus appearing to people around the world, but I have had no personal experience of this. A visual experience is very rare, even more than God revealing Himself audibly. In fact, Scripture warns us that our minds can deceive us in matters such as these (Col. 2:18).

In the Old Testament, when God appeared before someone, they were struck with overwhelming fear in almost every case (Moses, Isaiah, and Daniel). In each case, God revealed something of extreme significance. Even the apostles Paul and John were overcome when God appeared before them. Most of the time, God appears visually in dreams. This is also an area in which we must be very careful. While the Scripture gives examples of people to whom God appeared in dreams, it is not the most common way God speaks.

A Word from Others

This seems to happen mostly from the pulpit when God's Word is being taught. This has happened to me many, many times.

For someone to hear the voice of God does not place that person above anyone else. God's divine power and His direction is available to anyone. Ask Him to speak to you, then be quiet. Start with a minute or two of quiet time, then increase the time. At first, one minute may feel like ten, but soon you will get lost in listening, and your life will change forever.

I have now walked seventeen days on the trace, and I've covered 241 miles. God has been working with and in me this entire time. He has also been ministering to Sheryl, and our love is growing for each other. Now I am going to take off two days to rest and recover and will return to the trace early Monday morning to continue my walk with God.

Chapter 18

Listening Prayer

The first duty of love is to listen.
—Paul Tillich

July 21, 2014

On Monday morning, my eighteenth day of the walk, Sheryl drove me back to MM 241, south of Tupelo, where we left off in the heavy cold rain and traffic last Friday morning. That had been a miserable way to end the week, but now I am rested and ready to go.

Today's Reflections

During my quiet prayer time this morning, the Holy Spirit led me to think on the subject of prayer, especially listening prayer.

For many years, I ignored God. After my first divorce, I felt like a horrible sinner, and I began to pursue a relationship with God more diligently. Around the same time, I began to sense He was pursuing me. I began to pause near the end of my prayers and just be silent, meditate, and listen. I found the quieter I became, the better I could hear.

In 1990, I was convicted of the error in my ways as I reflected on what it means to ignore someone. Ignoring someone is the most egregious insult you can pay him. On the other hand, the sincerest form of respect is listening to another person and truly being present. Listening requires presence over talent, humility over ego, and a focus on others over self.

I had always been more interested in what I had to say than in listening. When engaged in conversation, I was often thinking about my next comment while the other person was still speaking. In doing so, I missed what was being said as well as the meaning. More importantly, when thinking of my response, I missed the underlying feelings shared through tone of voice, body language, or facial expressions. To make matters worse, I had a horrible habit of interrupting, cutting off the other person, or answering questions for others and drowning them out. It was disrespectful.

Listening is one of the elements of communication, just like talking, reading, and writing. Listening is the fundamental stance of a person of faith and a vital part of our faith journey. Our ability to hear God's direction is not a given for most people. It is a skill that must be applied and learned.

The apostle John quotes Jesus saying, "I have much more to say to you, more than you can now bear. But when he, the Spirit of truth, comes, he will guide you into all truth" (John 16:12–13).

In Deuteronomy 18:19, the Lord said, "I myself will call to account anyone who does not listen to my words that the prophet speaks in my name." And in 1 Corinthians 14:38, Paul says, "But if anyone ignores this, they will themselves be ignored." Hebrews 2:3 says, "How shall we escape if we ignore so great a salvation?"

I began to pay attention to the way I prayed. There was a genuine interest on my part to communicate better with God. At that point, most of my prayers sounded like this:

> Heavenly Father, thank You for the many blessings you've showered upon me. Dear Lord please help me to . . . Oh, Father I need . . . Please God open these doors for me . . . Thank You very much, Lord. See You later. Amen.

The first thing I noticed was that my prayer was one way—from me to God. If I ever heard from Him, I couldn't confirm it.

The next thing I noticed was that my prayer was all about me: the blessings I've received, the help I needed, the doors I wanted open.

Then I noticed my prayers often didn't sound like normal conversation but were juvenile, like the begging of a six-year-old.

I heard a great orator of a preacher admit from the pulpit one Sunday morning, "I probably don't spend more than three minutes a week in prayer with God. I am just too busy. If He speaks to me, it has to come when I am on the run, when I am least likely to pay attention." He may have been trying to appear humble, but his admission stunned me.

Many prayers are the symptoms of shallow, impersonal relationships with Jesus. We expect God to hear us, but we are missing the intimate dialogue possible between two best friends. After all, Jesus did call us His friends.

Can you imagine a relationship without communication? We talk with the people we love.

God tells us we are created to be in a relationship with Him.

Marriages that lack two-way communication grow stale. If I relate to Sheryl by giving her a daily account of things I've done or by telling her my thoughts but never ask about her activities, impressions, and feelings, then my relationship with her will be very one-sided. To have a personal relationship with Sheryl, I must listen to her and she to me.

Listening is a skill as well as an attitude of the heart. The same is true for our relationship with God. We talk to Him and must listen to Him. That is fulfilling the first commandment: "Love God with all your heart." If we struggle to really listen to people whom we can see, then we are going to find it impossible to listen to God, whom we cannot see.

When I began to work on listening, the direction in my life changed profoundly, and I began to hear God's voice in a variety of ways. I've learned that two-way communication in our earthly relationships is a clear pattern for communications with God.

Listening Skills

How do we develop the skills needed to listen to God?

The first skill I needed to develop is to be completely present. Silence is the training ground for the art of listening. Prayer is more than a matter of words; it is often at its best free from words, since our own chatter can prevent our listening.

The second skill was to listen to urgings in my conscious mind or checks in my spirit. When I sense even the slightest whisper of the Holy Spirit, I listen up.

After participating in one All-In men's discipleship group for two years, Bill McConnell and I were led to co-facilitate a new group. The All-In groups consist of eight to twelve men who perform daily homework and meet for two hours each week to disciple each other. Bill and I wondered where we'd recruit the men to participate with us.

Hal Hadden, the founder of CLC, which sponsors the All-In program, told us, "Pray and listen. God will bring men to you and lead you to the right men."

Instead of following Hal's advice, we used our sales backgrounds to draft lists of prospects to recruit. Within a few weeks, nine guys had committed to join us, then suddenly three dropped out, and we were back to six.

Losing the three got my attention. Finally, I heeded Hal's advice. I prayed, "Lord, please forgive me for not praying and seeking your guidance in recruiting our men. Please show us the way and lead us to the right guys." About an hour later, one of the committed six called and gave me a name of an interested guy. Then another called; then another. Within about two days, we were up to eleven men.

The third skill needed for listening is asking good questions. Probing questions prompt responses. Isaiah 8:19 says, "Should not a people inquire of their God?" The Scriptures are full of examples of people asking God questions. Matthew 7:7 says, "Ask and it will be given to you." God will answer our questions. Ask God about the choices you are considering. Ask about your problems. Ask for a warning when trouble is headed your way.

After posing a sincere question, I must suspend all my preconceived notions and human desires. The Holy Spirit responds in very surprising ways. Boy, was I surprised when He directed me on this walk!

Over time, we develop the ability to listen in silence. God continues to urge, direct, and speak long after we've got up from our devotional place. When God is talking or urging us, we must not interrupt or allow distractions. Psalm 46:10 says, "Be still and know that I am God." Being still implies a quietness of mind and spirit. My biggest challenge is not to allow my own desires and thoughts to get in the way of God's answer to my question. Too many days I try to hear God's voice on the run, then wonder why He doesn't speak. When I began practicing attentive and empathic listening, little by little I begin hearing God's voice.

Confirmation

Attentive, listening prayer must be connected with confirmation and specific action. God wants us to give him our praises, our struggles, and our questions. In return, He wants to give us counsel, encouragement, and consolation. This interaction becomes the fabric of our relationship. The more frequent and honest our dialogue is with Jesus, the more personal it becomes.

If we don't write down our messages from God, it is easy to stray to the right or the left. Satan does not have to make us do bad things. He just has to keep us busy doing good things to make us stray from the joy of carrying out our mission from the Lord. When God shares a mission or vision with us, He wants us to move forward on it!

Every Monday on this walk, I have been full of energy. It's a testament to the value of rest in recovery. With thirteen more miles behind me, I wrapped up my morning walk about 10:00 a.m. After a half hour in the pool, Sheryl and I enjoyed our time around Tupelo during the day and lunch at Harvey's Restaurant. Back on the walk at 6:10 p.m. for seven more miles, I wrapped up the day at MM 261, just a few miles from our hotel in Tupelo.

We toured the Chickasaw village exhibit at MM 261 to see exhibits showing the daily life of a native village that existed several hundred years ago.

Being over the halfway mark really feels good. After a quick supper, I jumped in the pool for another half hour and then off to bed for a satisfied sleep.

Chapter 19

God's Heart for Work

> *If our identity is in our work, rather than Christ, success will go to our heads, and failure will go to our hearts.*
> —Tim Keller

July 22, 2014

RISING SLOWLY ON DAY NINETEEN, I felt enormous gratitude to the Lord for giving me a renewed sense of physical strength. A few months ago, I felt washed up, over the hill, useless, and without value. Through these miles, God was letting me know I still had more to contribute and a strong body to keep moving forward.

Walking on the west side of the trace has been difficult the past two days, and my pace has slowed because of it. The shoulder has a deep slope, and the traffic is quite heavy, so I could not walk on the road.

Shortly after getting onto the trace, Russ Corley texted me, "I'm praying for your strength this morning." Russ had been my daily encourager, and he helped me set the pace for the day. Some days Russ texted me a prayer, other days a Bible verse or an encouraging word. What a great, great friend!

The weather was very cool at 5:30 a.m. just south of Tupelo as Sheryl dropped me off to begin at MM 261. I walked thirteen miles, finishing a few minutes after 10:00. I felt like I could have walked a few more miles but decided it was best to maintain a moderate pace.

To finish by August 1, it would be important to pace myself and walk thirteen miles each day without taking days off. That was beginning to seem like a huge challenge.

About 20 miles northwest of MM255 is Brice's Cross Roads National Battlefield Site where Confederate General Nathan Bedford Forrest waged a battle that is still studied in military schools worldwide. The exhibits show how an army can be greatly outmanned and still outwit the enemy. There is a museum on the site that describes Forrest's capture of a large cache of arms and 1,600 Union soldiers. Union losses were five times those of the Confederates, yet the Union army was three times the size of General Forrest's army.

Today's Reflections

During my quiet time this morning, the Holy Spirit urged me to revisit some work experiences and how they relate to my spiritual life.

Work has been my idol. I'm not sure if my dedication to work is from a place of greed or power or some deeper need, habit, or addiction. God blessed me with energy and physical strength, and work just became a way of life.

In addition to attending school and playing sports, I worked in my father's grocery store from the time I was six years old. I had summer jobs as an assistant on a Coca-Cola delivery truck and as a lifeguard at a swimming pool. We were shorthanded during much of my navy service, and I worked twelve hours on and twelve off. Upon discharge, I carried a full load at UT Knoxville while working a forty-hour week to pay my way. After graduation, I went to work for PricewaterhouseCoopers (PwC). Working only forty hours a week, I didn't know what to do with all the extra time, so I became very active in business clubs and politics and studied for my MBA.

After leaving PwC, I put my work life into high gear by working ninety to one hundred hours a week, very much as my father had done. I became CEO of a small publicly owned company with about two thousand shareholders. Over the next eight years, I was responsible for over forty acquisitions and divestitures, a proxy fight, regular Securities and Exchange Commission (SEC) filings, and reorganizing the company from a budget motel chain to a communication business. In 1983 when that job ended, I was physically exhausted, mentally burned out, and spiritually bankrupt.

In the late 1980s, I was first introduced to the concept of including God in my business life when I attended "Your Work Matters to God," a Doug Sherman video class. This was a 180-degree revelation for me. Prior to this class, I had compartmentalized my life: bucket one—work; bucket two—make money; bucket three—gain power and prestige; bucket four—family; and bucket five—God.

I learned we can serve and love our neighbors through work. I came to realize that God uses our work whether or not anyone tells us, "I thank God for what you are doing!" Through work we meet our own needs, those of our family, and others. If you are working to meet your legitimate needs, then you are fulfilling something important that God wants done in the world.

Through work we earn money to support our church, charities, and our children's education. As God gifts us, we are called to share that abundance with others who are in need. Sherman said every Christian, no matter his lifestyle, should use part of his or her money to meet the financial and material needs of others and, of course, tithe.

I've come to the realization that there is much more to life than work. Knowing I have a higher purpose is crucial. The Lord calls us to do everything to the glory of God.

Work as Devotion

We can love God through work if we do our work for Him. I try to turn my work into a temple of devotion to God. I feel like I am a minister doing full-time Christian service. Every Christian, wherever he is working, is in full-time Christian service.

For much of my life, "spirituality" had nothing to do with work. I thought spirituality meant praying (of which I did very little), attending Sunday school and church, and reading the Bible. John Paul II wrote of "a spirituality of work which will help all people to come closer, through work, to God, the Creator and Redeemer." Martin Luther King Jr. said:

> Whatever your life's work is, do it well. . . . If it falls on your lot to be a street sweeper, sweep streets like Michelangelo painted pictures, like Shakespeare wrote poetry, like

Troy Waugh

> Beethoven composed music; sweep streets so well that all the host of heaven and earth will have to pause and say, "Here lived a great street sweeper, who swept his job well."

Including spirituality in work engages both the owner and worker in trying to balance profits with the needs of employees and customers. At Rainmaker, we did our best to limit the international and domestic travel of our trainers and consultants to not interfere with their spiritual or family lives. Although we were far from perfect, we presented written Christian values to our employees and customers.

When a farmer plows with two mules, the normal yoke ensures the load is shared equally. A training yoke is used when teaching a young mule. The young mule learns from the more experienced one who pulls the entire load. The young mule only has to walk beside the older animal. In Matthew 11:29, Jesus commands us to take up His yoke. I think He is inviting us to take up his *training* yoke. I think Jesus is saying to us, "Just walk beside me. I'll carry the burden. I'll provide the power. I'll guide you down straight paths."

When we bear heavy loads or are faced with seemingly impossible tasks at work, we have God's promise that Jesus will not only be there with us, but He will carry the load.

Prayer and Work

Begin each day with quiet prayer. Many days my prayer is simply, "Dear God, this day is yours. Please, Lord, help me make this day praiseworthy for You." Most days, my quiet time is ten or fifteen minutes. During that time, I pray about things I expect that day and things I am worried or tempted about. Starting the day with the commitment to work for God can make difficult days satisfying.

Offer short prayers during the day. Sheryl is wonderful at this habit. When she can, she prays reverently on the porch in the early morning or evening and listens to the sounds of nature and the soft whispers of the Holy Spirit. I have tried to learn from her, as these regular short prayer breaks are her primary communications with the Lord. I keep my Bible, Christian books and music, and meaningful quotes around me to remind me to turn to God.

God's Heart for Work

Doing Your Best

Even if God is the only one who is a witness, do your best. As Martin Luther King Jr. said, "Whatever your life's work is, do it well."

Jesus said, "No one can serve two masters. Either he will hate the one and love the other, or he will be devoted to the one and despise the other. You cannot serve God and money" (Matt. 6:24).

John Wesley, founder of Methodism, had an unimaginably heavy work ethic. He traveled hundreds of thousands of miles, preached thousands of sermons, and started a global denomination. Wesley had incredible results as he worked in the power of the Holy Spirit.

Wesley challenged us to give all we can to the work of the kingdom after supporting our family. He advocated "gaining all we can" but not at the expense of life or health. He said we should not throw our precious talent away.

It's not what we do, it's how we do our jobs that matters to the Lord. If we sweep the floors in the school, play professional sports, or work in a business, we are serving Christ if we radiate love, joy, peace, patience, kindness, goodness, faithfulness, gentleness, and self-control—the fruit of the Spirit.

Remember, God uses ordinary people to do extraordinary things. God has taken me—an ordinary, common man—and has given me the power to do powerful things for Him! It is beyond my imagination that the Lord has given me the strength to carry out this walk.

I was back on the trace from 5:30 till 7:00 p.m. and covered another five miles. It felt very good to complete eighteen miles today. The lesson from this day's walk was to move my work into a subservient position in my life and ensure my relationship with Jesus is first.

Chapter 20

Forming New Habits

As a dog returns to his vomit, a fool returns to his folly.
—Proverbs 26:11

July 23, 2014

IN THE EARLY-MORNING HOURS MY heart was restless and very unsettled. The coffee was hot and wonderful as I sat down to visit quietly with the Lord. The Holy Spirit settled me down and helped me to focus on Him. Within a few minutes, my restlessness was soothed.

At 5:30 a.m., Sheryl took me to MM 279 for an early start to the day. We were north of Tupelo and a good drive from our hotel. I may have fallen too far behind to be finished by my birthday on August 1, as I was about twenty-five miles behind where I needed to be. With my hips and knees hurting and my blisters continuing to rise, each step sent sharp pains zinging up my legs. In the next few days, I had to decide whether to extend my walk or push harder each day.

About 9:00 a.m. I arrived at the Pharr Mounds at MM 286. On the panoramic ninety acres stand eight large mounds, the largest archeological site in the mid-South. These Native American burial grounds are breathtaking in their scope and mysterious in their gentle beauty. The mounds were built between AD 1 and AD 200 and include human remains along with earthly possessions.

Today's Reflections

New habits seemed to be the focus of the day, so as I left the hotel, I began to think and pray about forming new habits.

Someone once said, "The most difficult thing in life is to give up who you are for who you could become." Changing habits that may have served you well in childhood is difficult. It hasn't been easy for me, and I still slip and fail. But I am better today than I was a year ago. I was definitely better at the end of 2014 than I was at the beginning. That is growth for me. That is moving toward sanctification.

Some of the bad habits I have developed have been engraved on me for nearly seventy years. I don't want to smuggle the bad habits of my past into my future. When I begin to develop new habits, it's like pouring water in and forcing the old out.

Developing New Habits

Good habits make all the difference in life. If you have created good habits, you do the right things naturally. You don't have to think about it much. Over time, the new habit becomes a part of who you are and becomes ingrained into your behavior.

How am I going to modify my behavior to build these new habits and eliminate the bad ones? First, I must be aware of the ones I'd like to develop.

A Christian counselor, with whom I worked as a client, encouraged me to ask God to guide me in selecting the habits I wanted to build. He told me it may take several prayer sessions and many months. He had me write down those things I heard from God each day, especially during my dreams.

Three habits I have worked on and made some small progress in are being truthful, not lashing out in anger, and making a consistent golf swing.

Telling the Truth

When my youngest son, Brian, was about six years old, he asked me a question after church one Sunday morning. "Dad, why did you tell Ms. Johnson that she looked lovely today? Dad, Ms. Johnson is the ugliest woman in the church. I heard you say how ugly she is one time."

"Brian, I said that to make Ms. Johnson feel good."

"Well, Dad, don't you think Ms. Johnson knows she isn't pretty and all the people around know she is ugly?"

"You are so right, Brian" was my only possible response.

I realized telling lies to make someone feel good, to get out of an invitation, or to respond to the question "How are you?" all send a message that you are not to be trusted.

The counselor helped me to not label these habits as bad, not to repress them, but to call them up and literally thank them for their service to me when I was young. He encouraged me to present these protector habits to God and to thank Him for giving me strategies to protect myself when I was young.

I had to trust God would empower me to build new adult habits. After all, I was now an adult, and no one was going to physically harm me if I told the truth.

I have failed in always telling the truth many times, but I keep pecking away at it. Whenever I finish a day without telling untruths, I pat myself on the back, and the Holy Spirit rewards me with peace. At the end of a day in which I have intentionally lied, the Holy Spirit reminds me of my quest. I had to stop telling myself, You can't do it. The all-powerful God who created the universe and all that is within it will give me the strength.

By following the right strategies, we can all build good habits and make them stick. I like the phrase, "Do small well and regularly." For example, many people who haven't exercised in years decide they're going to start jogging for forty minutes five days a week. By setting the bar so high, failure is almost guaranteed.

At first, I set my goal so I was allowed one lie per day. I didn't begin by going to all those to whom I had lied and confessing my sins, which the 12-step program advises. Certainly that would have been the cleansing thing to do, but that was too big and too overwhelming. My feeling: Don't look back, you can't change it. Look forward, you can change that.

An even better strategy is to set the bar so low you practically trip over it. If you want to walk thirty minutes a day, make the decision to start walking for one minute a day. After a while you can raise the bar to two minutes a day, then three minutes, then four, and so on. It'll take you a while to build up to thirty minutes a day, but you'll get there. The most important thing is the habit, not the quantity.

As I built the new habit of telling the unvarnished truth, I had to take it one day at a time. I kept a log and reviewed the log each week for a month. Then I moved the bar up to three lies a week, then zero tolerance. After six months, I made a vow to correct any untruth I told as soon as I could. I still slip up once in a while, and I am very embarrassed when I do. But now I can truly say, "That is not me. It is not who I want to be. I have a commitment to the truth." But to change a lifelong engrained habit, I had to make things as *simple* as possible at the beginning and build from there.

I set my alarm every morning for 5:00 a.m. as a reminder to pray for truthfulness all day. I do not have the power to change this deeply ingrained habit on my own. The power of the Holy Spirit is the only power that can help me.

I worked on response strategies. When I am asked to attend a function to which I don't want to go, I simply say, "Oh, I cannot attend." I just leave it there.

When someone asks, "How are you?" I try to respond truthfully. "I'm struggling today" or "I feel really good" or "I'm worried about my friend today."

Rather than telling someone how beautiful or handsome he or she is, I say, "I love your smile" or "It is great to see you." There is always something truthful I can say to others.

Power and Willpower

Changing behaviors requires the power of the Holy Spirit and personal willpower. While the power of the Holy Spirit is limitless, personal willpower is a limited resource.

After several months, once the new habit is ingrained, it no longer requires as much willpower to sustain. Then I can get started on another new habit.

This year I am working on stopping before yellow lights and traveling no faster than five miles over the speed limit. I have been working on those two things all year, and I still slip up. Then a little voice says, *You blew it. Remember next time.* I sometimes set the speed control on the freeway just to keep my heavy foot from violating my new habit.

The more specific you are about what you're going to do, the more likely it is that you'll do it. The more often you do it, the more likely it is to turn into a habit.

The Anger Habit

I wanted to stop exhibiting anger toward people. I lost friends during angry outbursts when I said things I would never normally say. Unfortunately, my sons were adults before I really began working hard on altering this habit.

When my mother had chemotherapy treatments for cancer, she stayed with us for over a year. She did not feel well most of the time and would often complain about my sons disturbing her during the day, or she would tell me about something one of them had done to irritate her.

I came home from work one day and went into her bedroom to see how she was feeling. She immediately started telling me what Brian had done. I listened to her for a few minutes, then lost my temper. I marched out into the backyard, pulled up Brian by his belt and took him into my mother's bedroom. I took off my belt and whipped him right there in front of her, yelling at her, "Is this what you want me to do? Tell me what else he did! You want him punished, don't you?"

Of course, Brian was crying, she was crying, and I was sweating with fury. It was a horrible scene. In reality, I was whipping her, but I scarred Brian for life. I am so sad to tell this story.

With my counselor, I traced my anger back to my youth. I had learned to use anger after my parents used it on me. As a teenager, I used anger to thwart other boys from bullying me. I have exploded, many times violently, toward all my family members through the years.

My wife, Sheryl, is a very strong woman. She built a business, raised four daughters, and lived singly for twenty-five years. There have been many times when she disagreed with me and anger was my immediate impulse. However, with prayer and assistance from the Holy Spirit, I have been able to stop before I responded. I've learned to ask a question or two, then agree to consider her input. A few times, without praying or thinking, my responses have been angry, but mostly they have been thoughtful. Making the choice to respond thoughtfully has resulted in a better relationship with my wife.

Overcome Barriers

To deal with my explosive anger, I needed to remove two barriers: fatigue and impatience. As a workaholic, I never got enough rest and was always exhausted. The first thing I worked on was getting at least seven hours sleep each night, up from about four. To accomplish this, I had to settle my mind down long before bedtime, so I stopped watching disturbing TV shows. Having enough rest made me less irritable and a little more patient.

Still I had to focus on eliminating anger by praying for the Holy Spirit to eradicate it from me. Daily goals, a log, and steady prayer helped reduce the angry outbursts to almost none. I say almost none because every so often I literally lose control of my emotions and explode in anger.

During my training period for this walk, Sheryl complained about my irritability and anger bouts. Truth is, I was pushing beyond my physical limits and not resting enough. That lasted for two months, but once I began the walk on June 30, most of that anger subsided.

Learning about triggers and how to recognize them was a crucial step in changing this habit. One of the biggest triggers for me was when someone disagreed with me. That challenged me, put me on the defensive, and often caused me to strike back with greater force. I had to learn it was okay when someone disagrees with me. I needed to take that as learning new information, respect it, and try to understand it. I had to learn the habit of restating what someone said that I disagreed with and asking questions around it before responding. Just restating the other person's argument often helped me see their wisdom and helped me grow.

Celebrate Success

To make a new habit stick, I reward myself. When I was writing my first book some twenty years ago, I set daily goals. If I met that goal, I rewarded myself. In those days after the goal was met, it was a round of golf or an ice cream, a piece of chocolate, a walk in the forest, or a swim in the pool—something positive and fun. I learned giving myself a reward after performing the new action correctly reinforced my brain in a positive manner.

What gets rewarded gets repeated. Rather than beat myself up for failing, I found that associating pleasure with the new habit helps it take hold.

Forgive Yourself

I had to learn to forgive myself when I failed. After a failure I confessed the failure to God and then walked away from it. I admitted my guilt but didn't allow it to turn into shame. The difference between guilt and shame is huge. By immediately forgiving myself for the transgression, the guilt did not fester.

I have adapted the motto, "To err is human; to blame someone else is even more human."

Give It Time

I had to commit to a six-month challenge. Thirty, sixty, or ninety days is just not enough to change a deeply ingrained habit. This is hard work. I don't believe in the common twenty-one-day training plan. Maybe I am slow, but it just does not work for me.

For me, the best time to pray about and work on changing a habit is first thing in the morning. In the morning when I have my quiet time with the Lord, I have the most energy and personal willpower. I have learned I can become what I consistently do every day.

This being Wednesday, I walked thirteen miles in the morning and rested in the afternoon. I had covered thirty-eight miles the previous two days. Sheryl picked me up at MM 292 at about 10:00 a.m. I enjoyed the rest of the day reflecting on building new habits and writing in my journal.

Chapter 21

Goals, Plans, and Prayer

With God, there's always an appointed time for things, and when you put Him first, trust in His timing, and keep the faith, miracles happen!
—Germany Kent

July 24, 2014

WALKING ON DAY TWENTY-ONE BEGAN at 6:00 a.m. at MM 292 with the sun just peeking over the horizon. This Thursday morning my blisters were growing and my legs and hips were tiring. I covered nine miles and felt myself slowing down considerably.

After the morning walk, we moved from Tupelo to Belmont, Mississippi. With friends coming to walk, we planned to stay in Belmont over the weekend.

Belmont, incorporated in 1908, is a lovely town with a population of about 2,000. Its name means beautiful mountain. We checked in to the Belmont Hotel, built in 1924, and found the facility needing a little TLC. After dinner in the Hallmark Restaurant, a wonderful little "meat-and-three" diner, we enjoyed sitting in the lobby of the Belmont, with its tall ceilings and vintage wallpaper, and chatting with other guests who were biking the trace. Sheryl said the ornate heavy draperies in the hotel lobby, lounge, and dining room reminded her of the days of Miss Scarlett.

I was determined to push on, so Sheryl took me back to MM 301 to cover some more ground before dark. From 5:30 to 7:00 p.m., I was able to walk four more miles before crashing for the day. My flat, musty pillow and body pains kept me from sleeping very well.

I did some research and found rooms in Florence, Alabama, for the weekend. New owners have purchased and refurbished this wonderful hotel making it a wonderful stop along the Trace.

Sheryl and I were looking forward to our friends joining us. Many people said they would join us, but these wonderful friends were following through. Rev. Russ Corley and his wife, Jackie, and Buster Wolfe Jr. and his wife, Darlene, had been staying in touch with us the entire trip. Russ was my daily coach.

Today's Reflections

As I woke up, my mind focused on my goal of completing this walk a week from now. For most of my life I have been a planner and a goal setter. Some of my plans and goals have been achieved; some have failed. One of the major revelations of this trip has been that the Lord has blessed with excellent outcomes those plans for which I prayed and listened. It has been clear the plans I have made on my own were the ones that failed. In some cases, the plans not prayed for not only failed, many of them led to calamities beyond my imagination.

Noted business guru, Peter Drucker, taught that a successful person must concentrate scarce resources on the greatest opportunities and results. He believed in doing the right things, and doing them with intensity and excellence. The surest way to achieve a goal is to prioritize everything you do. But Drucker missed the most important force multiplier of the ages—the power of God.

Most days in business, I bolt into the to-do list ready to tackle my top priorities. I am continually improving in offering that list to the Holy Spirit. Refusing to offer up my list and be open to alternative actions is a surefire way to live a mediocre life. We all have things to do, places to go, and people to see. I must be open to the Holy Spirit changing my plans. The top item every day on my to-do list must be to listen and yield to the Holy Spirit.

As I have been slowing down my pace from pain and exhaustion, I have been thinking about my goal of completing the walk on the 444 miles of the Natchez Trace by August 1. Having covered over 300 miles and now slowing down, I am praying about a variety of options:

1. Push hard to complete the walk by August 1. This is my human instinct.
2. Keep walking and complete the walk as I am able, even though I may be a few days late. This seems like a failure, although I know it is not.
3. Stop walking now, heal, and resume walking when I feel physically able. This would be an even larger failure than #2, although it still would be a completion.
4. End the walk now. Such a thought must be banished from my brain. Failing to complete this walk when God has called me to accomplish it would be letting Him down, letting myself down, and letting down my friends.

An old maxim in strategy is to plan carefully but rip up the plan once engaged in battle. In May and June, as I was preparing for this trip, I prayed daily for God's guidance in planning. God set the goal for me and seems to have left the tactics to me.

God's Plans

In my consulting and training business over the last twenty-five years, I have assisted with and consulted in the development and implementation of hundreds of plans. My most valued business offering includes helping business leaders develop a mission (purpose), vision (future state), and values.

I am realizing I have failed to bring God into many of those business plans. How could I have left out the most powerful force in the universe? Today this is the aha moment for me.

> For I know the plans I have for you, declares the Lord, plans for welfare and not for evil, to give you a future and a hope. Then you will call upon me and come and pray to me, and I will hear you. You will seek me and find me, when you seek me with all your heart.
> (Jer. 29:11–13 ESV)

God has a road map for all our lives. His plan is for us to become better disciples for His kingdom. Looking back, I can see where God's hand was at work when my plans failed. Although I rely on God's Word, it's still easy to wonder, Where should I live? Who should be my friends? What work am I to do? *Who am I to marry?* God's plans are not so much about those specifics as they are about developing character, integrity, faith, love, and being sanctified.

My own experience has been that God will reveal His road map for us if we listen. In some cases He will give us the long view, while in others He doesn't share all the details, as He wants us to step out in faith, hour by hour. When God whispers, "I know the plans I have for you," His words relax me. But wouldn't you love to get a look at those plans? The tension isn't does God know? The concern is I want to know!

First, His plans are for our welfare. As God looks down our fourscore of years of time, His plans are for our well-being, fulfillment, prosperity, and peace.

Second, His plans for us are not for evil. When I live contrary to God's plan, I pay a price by being separated from Him. God's plans take us away from self to serve Him and others.

Third, God tells us we have a future and a hope, both immediately and eternally. The biblical definition of hope is *a* "confident expectation of something better tomorrow." When our hope is in God, He'll always deliver. The past doesn't matter; better things are in store.

In 2 Peter 1:5, Peter challenges us to persevere. He says God has given us all the divine power we need and provides us instructions for developing character.

Mission, Values, and Vision

In my strategic-planning work, mission permeates everything we do with strategy and defines our fundamental purpose. Understanding the purpose for our long- and short-term plans is crucial. A mission statement answers the question, what do we do?

My mission is to model a Christian life. God reveals that mission to me when I listen to Him.

Mission connects the present and future—our vision. Our daily objectives should align with our mission and be constantly compared to ensure that we're on track toward our vision and within the bounds of our values. Mission and values exist both today and in the future.

Values define our guidelines. Values such as integrity, excellence, and teamwork define what we stand for, the kind of people we want to associate with, etc. Values are self-selected and require careful definition.

Vision is only true in the future. Vision is not true today, only when you arrive at a new location. Vision is a long-term view and defines the desired or intended future state of a plan. A vision should be clearly stated so you know when you've arrived. In my experience, a person without a vision simply floats along aimlessly, vulnerable to the winds of the circumstances.

My vision is completing my walk and having dinner with family and friends at the Loveless Café. The Loveless is located within a quarter mile and in sight of Nashville's ramp to the Natchez Trace Parkway where I will complete the walk. My vision was not true one month ago, but it will be true within the next two weeks.

Florence Chadwick twice swam the twenty-three-mile-wide English Channel. She was an American distance swimmer who attempted the twenty-six-mile swim between the California coastline and Catalina Island. During her swim, Chadwick traveled with a team whose job was to keep an eye out for sharks and be prepared to assist in the event of unexpected cramps, injury, or fatigue.

Roughly fifteen hours into her swim, a thick fog set in, clouding Chadwick's vision and confidence. Her mother happened to be in one of the boats at the time that Chadwick relayed to her team that she didn't think she could complete the swim. She swam for another hour before deciding to call it quits. Chadwick discovered if she'd continued on for just another mile, she would have reached Catalina Island.

Many people quit a dream on the brink of its realization. It's when the challenges feel the most daunting that we're often closer to our destination than we think we are. If we can paddle through a little fog, we'll discover that haze eventually gives way to a sense of clarity.

Planning cannot foretell exactly how events will evolve. Regular adjustments to the strategic plan have to be made. Even an airplane on a well-charted course from New York to Paris continually readjusts its direction as it flies through buffeting winds and weather systems.

I have had to readjust my plans almost every day. This is why daily prayer is essential to living a life with Jesus.

As we end our day, I feel grateful to God for giving me strength to continue to walk with Him, mile after mile, day by day. With 305 miles behind us, wrapping up at 7:00 p.m. on Thursday, July 24, is a cause for praise and celebration. Thank you, Lord.

Chapter 22

God and Money

*Money never stays with me. It would burn me if it did.
I throw it out of my hands as soon as possible,
lest it should find its way into my heart.*
—John Wesley

July 25, 2014

I AWOKE ON FRIDAY WITH a sense of peace with Sheryl beside me and the blessing of friends coming to walk with me.

Sheryl drove me a bit south, over the Tennessee River and across the Mississippi state line, to MM 305. About an hour and a half into my morning hike, I encountered Bear Creek Mound at MM 309. The area around the mounds, which date back nearly 9,000 years, was occupied by indigenous people until about AD 1300. I took a short break to feel connected to the 10,000 years of human history that lay before me.

Today's Reflections

The Lord has impressed upon me to think about money and see if I can clarify my beliefs on money, reconcile my concepts with those presented by Jesus, and modify my ways regarding money if I find opportunities to improve.

Money has been a motivator for me from my youth. I've worked many hours for money, chased many business deals for money, and made good and bad decisions going after money. God has blessed me with money, and I have committed many sins involving money. Some of my most colossal failures have been the manner in which I have handled money.

What should I be doing with it? That is what the Holy Spirit seems to be urging today.

One of my greatest sins has been greed. For years it enslaved me. I recall being relatively poor when I was young and telling my parents, "I'm going to be a millionaire by the time I'm forty." From that point on, I made many choices based on money. When I was a kid, I took music lessons and played a few instruments. When I told one of my teachers that I wanted to be a professional musician, she said, "You'll never make any money," so I dropped that idea like a hot potato.

When I qualified for the Navy SEALs program at eighteen, my company commander said, "You'll never make as much money as if you went to a trade school and joined the submarine service." I immediately dropped the idea of the SEALs and went for the money.

Jesus and Money

Jesus talks about money quite a bit more than many sins on which we usually focus.

The more I have focused on Jesus's advice on money, the better my financial life has been. Nearly half the parables of Jesus deal with possessions or money. A large percentage of the Gospels deals with possessions and money. The Scriptures include about five hundred verses each on prayer and faith, while more than two thousand verses speak to possessions and money. Perhaps the reason the Bible puts such an emphasis on money is because Jesus said in Matthew 6:21, "For where your treasure is, there your heart will be also."

Jesus warns how dangerous the pursuit of money can be:

> No one can serve two masters. Either you will hate the one and love the other, or you will be devoted to the one and despise the other. You cannot serve both God and money. (Matt. 6:24)
>
> Again I tell you, it is easier for a camel to go through the eye of a needle than for a rich man to enter the kingdom of God. (Matt. 19:24)

> Watch out! Be on your guard against all kinds of greed; a man's life does not consist in the abundance of his possessions. (Luke 12:15)

The apostle Paul said, "For the love of money is a root of all kinds of evil. Some people, eager for money, have wandered from the faith and pierced themselves with many griefs" (1 Tim. 6:10).

Financial Peace

In 1991, Dave Ramsey, a popular radio host, author, and speaker who teaches people how to manage money, gave me my first common sense tutorial on money. Dave and his family attended church with my family, and I learned of his early struggles with money. Dave wrote his first book, *Financial Peace,* from his experiences in financial crisis. He taught me the wisdom around Proverbs 22:7, "The debtor is a slave to the lender." Dave Ramsey advised eradicating debt, challenged us to manage money so it wouldn't manage us, and lower my living style to fit eighty percent of my income or less.

As a result, my wife and I were motivated to get out of debt and refocus our attitudes toward the acquisition of stuff. Living debt-free has given me freedom and removed the stress of money from my life. I wish I had understood and obeyed God's instructions on money years ago.

I don't believe Jesus or His apostles commanded that I should stay poor, but both Jesus and Paul spoke against the evils of making money my idol.

I previously viewed money in a mathematical sense: buy stock on margin, use debt for consumer items, and seek the highest possible return without regard to the risk. I had borrowed the most possible in buying a house. I had car payments and bank credit cards with high balances, along with gasoline and department store charge cards. Using Ramsey's principles, I lived on less and paid all this off within a few years.

Extinguishing worry from my financial life was huge. Being at peace and contented is a more biblical goal than maximizing profits and returns. In fact, In 1 Timothy 6:6, Paul relates contentment to godliness.

Troy Waugh

Get Rich Quick

When I was overextended financially, I tended to take bigger risks. The people who can afford it least are the ones who spend the most on lottery tickets. The lottery has been called a tax on the poor and the ignorant who can't do math. The truth is that the lottery is a rip-off instituted by politicians who want more of your money to waste. Studies show that eighty percent of lottery ticket buyers make less than $20,000 per year and live in lower-income zip codes. The get-rich-quick notion is highly tempting to someone deep in debt. Yes, the vagaries of the market are always unpredictable, and most times the risks I took resulted in huge losses. Those losses caused me to borrow more, worry more, drink more, think recklessly, and act sinfully.

Money will buy a nice house, but not a home. Money will buy a bed, but not a good night's sleep; a companion, not a friend; fun, not joy.

Tithing = One-Tenth

During the period in my life when I overspent and overborrowed, I balanced the books by leaving off tithing and giving.

In 1985, I changed the manner in which I earned, spent, and borrowed money. When I returned to tithing, somehow my earnings grew, and I began to accumulate some money for savings and retirement funds. While I will never be rich by some standards, God has blessed me so I am in the top five percent of the world in wealth. Probably you are as well. This method of living has also allowed me to find joy in giving beyond my tithe, which is an amazingly good feeling. "'Tis more blessed to give than receive" is a maxim that has universal truth. I truly feel blessed that I can tithe and give to the work of God's kingdom.

There is a humorous Bernadette Peters line in the movie *The Jerk* when she and her husband had to give back all the money they had made. She said, "I don't care about the money, I just want the stuff." It's interesting that one of the most profitable industries in America is storage facilities where people store the stuff that won't fit in their homes.

Paul exhorts us to not buy more stuff but be content with what we have. Removing my focus on buying more stuff helps me to create joy for myself and others.

Pure Greed

Even though I had dramatically changed my money habits in 1985, one of the biggest mistakes of my financial life took place in 2001. Without praying and without any guidance from the Lord, I loaned a family member a large amount of money. I was hungrily counting all the profits this loan would make. I was very prideful that I was a big-deal investor owning a large piece of another business.

My pride and greed came crashing down month after month as I saw the business suck up cash and lose market share and employees. Within a year, all that loaned and invested money was gone, and it had caused a malaise within our family. I was spending more and more time with the troubled investment. Over the next eight years, I spent hundreds of thousands of dollars defending litigation surrounding that investment. Looking back, I realized I didn't pray about it. I did not follow God's and Dave Ramsey's advice to neither a borrower nor lender be. I loaned that money purely out of a sense of greed, and the two thousand-year-old Scripture came true in my life.

The main way greed enslaves us is through deception. It didn't march right up to me and say, *I am greed, and I want to control your life.* Satan used the desire for money to appeal to my love of self and my greed. This deception affected me in several ways:

1. Greed deceived me by gradually becoming my master. For the next eight years, I was a slave to greed.

2. Greed deceived me by making money my focus for power, status, and happiness. Greed can deceive us if money is our hope for security.

I once heard Zig Ziglar tell the story of a businessman who encountered a genie. The genie granted him one wish. He requested a copy of *The Wall Street Journal* one year in the future. As he was studying the stock prices and planning the huge profits he would make, he discovered his own picture, name, and bio in the obituaries. Suddenly, that potential financial killing lost its significance.

Free from Slavery

When I finally became free from the slavery of greed and debt, I realized many benefits:

1. Spiritual

I have become a better, more faithful steward of God's money. After all, we will not be able to take the money with us. We are only able to use it while we are on the earth. Pleasing God is the primary motive for developing peace and self-control in financial matters. I have the satisfaction of knowing I am laying up treasures in heaven as I am now able to give tithes and offering to support God's work. When I was feeding the debt kitty, I couldn't handle money God's way.

2. Relational

My family was free from the tension over finances. Money is one of the leading causes of marital disputes and divorce. The pressures in family life are substantial without having money quarrels. Teaching my children about handling money is one of the most important aspects of parenting.

3. Personal

When we are debt-free, the anxiety around money is removed, and peace comes in its place. Jesus talked about the anxiety that results from living for things—our worry about moths, rust, and thieves (Matt. 6:19–33). When I am in debt, the pressure of who to pay first and how to keep my creditors at bay causes great anxiety.

This morning I walked twelve miles with good energy and an eye toward another good twelve miles tomorrow. It took me four hours to cover the twelve miles this morning, a little slower than my normal 3.5 mph pace.

Chapter 23

A New Career

In order to be a mentor, and an effective one, you must care. You don't have to know how many square miles are in Idaho, the chemical makeup of chemistry, or of blood, or water. Care about what you know and care about the person you're sharing with.
—Maya Angelou

July 26, 2014

SATURDAY MORNING WAS A GLORIOUS morning. Our friends Russ and Jackie Corley and Buster and Darlene Wolfe joined us last night in Florence, Alabama. After walking yesterday from Mississippi into Alabama, Russ and I began our morning at MM 317. (There are about thirty miles of the trace in Alabama, 310 miles in Mississippi, and about one hundred in Tennessee.)

Over coffee this morning, the Holy Spirit urged me to talk with Russ and Buster about Missions Development International. They have both had course changes in their careers and would be good sounding boards.

Walking and talking with Russ is like being with a disciple of Jesus. He is full of wisdom and care. We talked about many of the issues with which I had been grappling over the last month, and Russ provided deep insights for me.

The stories of Moses and Paul and others reveal that they spent time alone with God preparing for their ultimate mission.

This has happened with Russ. He earned his PhD in divinity and became associate minister of one of the largest churches in Nashville. Following his departure from that ministry role, Russ has spent the last twenty-five years serving God through Encouragement Ministries, a ministry with little fanfare or exposure.

During our walk, Russ shared that he is helping fill in as interim minister for Madison Church of Christ. Subsequent to our walk, the elders asked Russ to become their full-time minister. God is using Russ in a magnificent way in leading one of the largest churches in Metropolitan Nashville.

Later in the morning, Sheryl and the rest of our merry band of friends joined up, and we walked across the magnificent Tennessee River together. The beautiful morning sunshine on the mile-long walk across the river was awe inspiring. On the north side, we held a big celebration together with songs, high fives, and some chocolate milk. Reaching MM 329, I had twelve more miles covered.

Buster and Darlene Wolfe have become our very best and most trusted friends and are two of the most loving and giving people we know. We have traveled the world with them, and we often dine together. They quietly have helped many people through difficult times by listening, counseling, and supporting. Sheryl and I feel complete when our friends are with us.

Today's Reflections

For the last three weeks, I have been looking back over my life trying to make sense out of it. Sipping the intoxicating drink of my careers came at great cost and dulled my senses and my soul. During these last few weeks, I have laughed, cried, and been embarrassed and proud, all in the same hour. I've been thankful and regretful many times over the same issue. God has shown me how my dedication to work has animated me and simultaneously strangled my soul. Now I am getting a sense that God wants to begin to direct me toward a new future.

A few weeks ago, I met with Steve Lorenz and Marti Scudder to talk about volunteering with Missions Development International (MDI). I met them through the volunteer work I did with Today's Choices, the ministry in Ghana, West Africa, that developed the Sweetwater House, the home for young women for which I collected books. Over these last few months, I thought about working with MDI.

Steve and Marti were mentoring the leaders of the ministry in Ghana, and I was fascinated by their work. Steve and Marti had founded MDI in 1996 and volunteered their Christian-based mentoring services to leaders in ten countries. After our brief encounter, the seed had been planted for an ongoing relationship with Steve, Marti, and MDI.

My son Brian shared with me some of the difficulties that a growing ministry with which he was involved was experiencing. In early 2014, I had lunch with the leaders of this organization and was captivated by their dedication to the Lord's ministry and their present difficult circumstances.

The ministry was not attracting enough money to pay the bills. The founders were working night and day. They loaned their organization the money to pay the bills. The dozen employees were working from the founder's home. The clients were served from the founder's home from 9:00 in the morning till 9:00 at night. The founders were prisoners in their own home, were emotionally spent, doubting God, and on the verge of total burnout. Burnout is a sad statistic of many parachurch ministries—over seventy percent experience burnout.

Some of my most satisfying work has been helping leaders think through their purpose and their goals for the future. I came to believe that MDI could be of great service to these leaders. Today God impressed upon me to pray for them and how and if I should be involved.

Preparation for Service

The consulting work I did with Rainmaker was great preparation for working with MDI. However, the mentors at MDI take their work to a much deeper level than I had experienced with accounting firms. MDI mentors become close friends with their leader clients, where I separated friendship and consulting.

The most striking difference between MDI mentoring and my Rainmaker work is that MDI Mentors become prayer warriors with our clients. Meetings are opened and closed with prayer. Sometimes we even break in the middle of a meeting to pray. Calling on the power of the Holy Spirit was a normal part of everything we do.

In looking back on my Rainmaker work, I wish I had prayed over and with my client leaders. While I generally prayed for God's guidance, I rarely took the challenges of my clients to God. In retrospect, I had built a business that was God-inspired, but I had not brought Him into the minute details. I began to realize how shortsighted I had been.

After feeling God urging me to move forward with MDI, I made an appointment to visit Steve and Marti to discuss my potential involvement with them. Although almost all their work had been performed by the founders of MDI along with their executive director, they were considering adding volunteer mentors to their team. They were all very transparent with me, sharing their financial information, their successes, failures, and what they called their DNA.

A DNA of Dependence on God

The main element of MDI's DNA—or values—was their commitment and practice of leaning on God for His leadership and guidance. That value was clear in all their meetings with me as well and when I observed their work with Today's Choices many months earlier.

Steve and Marti adhere to a leader-first approach in which the leader's health, direction, and decision-making are paramount. They believe healthy leaders need mentoring and care in order to perform their functions in the kingdom. The MDI team are great listeners and lead their mentoring work with probing questions to help the leaders think deeply. While they affirm the leaders, they help him or her interpret the logic and feasibility of their thinking and directions.

Order Out of Chaos

I'm so grateful that during my twilight years, God has restored my vitality for service, with more balance and perspective than ever before.

Since joining the MDI team, I've worked with dozens of committed Christian leaders and have had a front row seat to the glorious workings of God. I watched God bring order to one organization experiencing chaos. Heather Karls, the executive director of MDI, and I helped the leaders develop a strategic plan that included a well-reasoned mission, vision, and set of values. Once the vision for the future was established, a set of prioritized objectives was agreed upon. A key objective was to bring the board together as a cohesive unit, praying and working together toward a common vision. Another was to cure the financial struggles.

About two months before the group's annual fund-raising event, the board agreed to a prayer quest for forty days. This took place every morning at 7:00 a.m. and lasted only five minutes. It got the board praying together for the success of the fund-raiser and the cohesiveness of the board members. God brought this group of men and women together as a solid board with a cohesive purpose and vision. In addition, the fund-raising dinner achieved seventy-five percent more than expected in donations and cured the financial shortage. Within a short time, God answered our prayers and the board's. Never in my life had I seen an organization achieve such miraculous results in such a short time.

Having mentored a few Christian leaders now, I have witnessed a fairly common element of spiritual warfare that takes place. Christian leaders are called to this work because they have a heart for God and for His people. Their work is often difficult and exhausting, whether it's serving the homeless, witnessing to the lost, or caring for the spiritual and mental illnesses that plague our society. They often have very little energy left to replenish bodies and souls.

After serving long hours and days, many leaders lessen their quiet time with the Master and work themselves into ministry burnout. Exhausted, with lessened prayer discipline, leaders often lose their perspective and sense of priority. Satan pulls them away from the mission God had placed on their hearts. Soon they become scattered trying to please others and so busy they fizzle out during their primary mission.

Many times, if we can encourage our leaders to return to the prayer life they had when the ministry began, God will lead them back to the ministry He had in mind for them.

After our glorious morning walk with our friends, Sheryl and I went home for Saturday night before returning to Lawrenceburg, near the trace and our next week's walking adventures.

We were excited to be at church with our friends and to hear a terrific sermon by our new pastor, Betty Proctor. Pastor Betty, who grew up in Israel where her parents served as missionaries to the Palestinians, came to our church in June and has been a blessing to our little congregation in Leiper's Fork. A recent graduate of Asbury Theological Seminary near Lexington, Kentucky, she had been a schoolteacher before becoming a minister.

That day I sat down on the hill beside my house to think about the Lord's wonderful kindness to me in the twilight of my life. I thought about how I have taken the Lord for granted, not loved Him with my whole heart, yet His love has been unfailing for me. My morbid imagination projected me into the coffin where I will lie when the Lord calls me home. I imagined some of my friends in the church would be sad, and some would be glad knowing I no longer was tormented by regrets, wonderings, and doubt.

Sunday evening, July 27, to make some additional progress, I walked for an hour and covered three miles.

Chapter 24

Idols Take the Stage

When people say, "I know God forgives me, but I can't forgive myself," they mean that they have failed an idol, whose approval is more important than God's.
—Tim Keller

July 28, 2014

IN THAT SPACE BETWEEN DEEP sleep and the stillness of the day's first awareness, I felt the nearness of the Lord. Awareness of His presence caused me to mull over the many times I have not sensed this closeness, times when other things have seized the top spot. Today I rise excitedly, expectantly, and in the mood for reflection and redemption.

To begin the day, we drove north across the magnificent Tennessee River to MM 332. Still inside Alabama, the morning portion of the day began before daybreak at 5:00 a.m. and ended about 10:00, moving me fourteen miles in five hours into the state of Tennessee.

Today's Reflections

Today my focus was on my life's priorities, especially the idols in my life. The Holy Spirit wants to crush the idols of my life that have consumed my spirit and interfered with my joy. If you ventured down the halls of my heart, you would be astonished that God can still work in my life. Priorities placed above my God are idols that I have molded to replace my Creator's position. Such an analysis has the possibility of taking me back to the shame in my life, the bad choices, and dark places.

Dark Places

As we peel back the layers of our lives,
we see and hear
and sometimes understand
the gifts we have stored in the basement
from that joyful time
are not gone but have been wrapped
in brown paper and stored
back in the darkest places
until we can love again,
until we can share again,
until we can look in the mirror again
and embrace our own image,
our own passions,
our own affections
and release the shackles of
those tears and fears that have held us captive
for too long.

The Old Testament is full of stories of how God's people rejected Him to worship statues or idols. While Moses was communing with God, the people turned to idols. During Elijah's life, King Ahab led Israel to worship Baal. Idol worship brought ruin. After Elijah taunted the idols' priests, he asked God to send fire to the altar. Through this demonstration of the power of God, the people returned to Him.

The second of the Ten Commandments says, *"You shall not make for yourself an idol in the form of anything in heaven above or on the earth beneath or in the waters below. You shall not bow down to them or worship them"* (Ex. 20:4–5).

An idol isn't just a tangible piece of wood or stone like a Buddha or an Asherah pole. An idol can be money, sex, power, or even our jobs or family members. An idol could be a sport or a hobby. Anything that consumes our time or resources, whether tangible or intangible, is an idol.

When I try to draw my motivation and strength from something other than God—that is an idol. Most times that idol has been my selfishness. Idolatry can include material images, relationships, a career, money, or an addiction. It could be a mindset that isolates us from the love of God.

Anything qualifies as an idol when we place godlike values on something that doesn't have the power of God, the Creator of the universe. Whenever we spend inordinate amounts of time worshiping the created rather than the Creator, we lose our connection with real wisdom and power. We must remove the idols so only the Lord remains as the primary object of our worship.

John Maxwell said, "Show me your calendar, and I will tell you about what you value most." I've found many of my priorities are not actually listed on my calendar. They take place in the dark places, the hidden places, the places I don't want anyone to see. His comment challenged me to be more honest and to invest more time with the Lord.

Another way to express this is "Where you spend your time is what you value the most." Jesus said, "For where your treasure is, there your heart will be also" (Matt. 6:21).

Self

The source of all sin is placing "me" in front of God. Serving myself—my wants, my needs, my desires, and my cravings—has always been my stumbling block—my idol. Truly, I vacillate between placing God at the top of my priorities and placing myself there.

During church services and my quiet time, I place God at the top and clean up my heart for short periods. Worshiping with others where God is present cleanses my soul for brief periods of time. But when greed, pride, work, and sexual immorality have consumed my time, God hasn't been the object of my worship. I was worshiping *myself. My* unstated mantra has been I'm most important; what I want comes first. "God is my co-pilot" should be rephrased, "I am God's co-pilot."

Ephesian 5:5 says, "For of this you can be sure: No immoral, impure or greedy person—such a person is an idolater—has any inheritance in the kingdom of Christ and of God."

Gratifying my cravings instead of pleasing God has been my stumbling block. My workaholism, deceitfulness, adultery, and money focus nearly ruined my life. It's only by the shed blood of Jesus that this horrible human being can be accepted into the kingdom of the Lord.

I found it easy to use the temporary achievements of career accomplishment to give my life meaning and significance—the very qualities only God can supply—and to occupy the center of my calendar and worship.

Family

With my career as my idol, I made myself an idol and placed my wants in front of God, in front of my wife, in front of my children, and in front of my neighbors and friends.

One of my biggest failures in life has been to outsource the spiritual training of my sons to the church. I feel like a huge failure in the most important thing God asks a man to do—to raise up children in the way they should go. It is only by the grace of God through Jesus Christ that my guilt and shame have been sealed on the cross.

Sadly, I recall many times landing in a city in another state, renting a car, and driving by a youth baseball game while lamenting missing my own boys' games that night. What did I give up for a few pieces of silver? Yet there were many wonderful days and weeks with my boys: vacations, boating trips, scouting, football, and soccer.

Despite the dark places my soul has experienced, today God has given me hope that I do have strength remaining through Him to attain what He wants for me.

Today we stayed in Lawrenceburg, Tennessee, with our friends, Chunky and Gail Moore. Gail and Sheryl have been friends since their high school days. It feels so good to be in a home environment rather than in a motel. Sheryl drove me back to MM 346 at 5:30, and I was able to add six more miles to near Collinwood, Tennessee. We are both enthused that with 352 miles behind us, we now only have ninety-two miles to go! Praise God! The energy on Monday helped pull me across twenty miles today. Thank you, Lord.

Chapter 25

Choices Make a Life

Everyone makes mistakes in life, but that doesn't mean they have to pay for them the rest of their lives. Sometimes good people make bad choices. It doesn't mean they are bad. It means they are human.
—Anonymous

July 29, 2014

TUESDAY, THE TWENTY-FIFTH DAY OF the walk, I spent considerable time salving and wrapping my blisters and carefully putting on my socks and shoes. With the warmth of my coffee and the predawn darkness outside, this was a good time to talk with the Lord.

As first light wiped away the stars giving the gift of a new day, I breathed in the fresh, cool air as Sheryl drove me to MM 352. I felt my body was breaking down; my hips and knees were throbbing, ankles were swollen, and feet burning. Gingerly, I stepped out in strong faith and the sheer power of the Lord. Each step reminded me of His pain and brought me closer to Him. I was reminded that I was to rely on Him to carry me through.

The fresh air felt almost frigid, and I jogged the first fifteen minutes to warm myself and numb the pain. Then for fourteen new miles I was just feeling, watching, loving, and walking softly into the cool breath of God.

Troy Waugh

Today's Reflections

Today the Holy Spirit led me to think and pray about choices: choices I have made and choices I will make in the future. My part is trusting God to know the right path and just stepping out in faith.

I am a quick decision maker and have lived by the mantra *I'm often wrong but never in doubt*. A golf pro once analyzed me in ten minutes. He said, "You approach golf like you approach life—with your hair on fire. My goal is to slow you down, help you to think and play better golf."

I've always believed if I made a wrong choice, I could make another choice to correct the error. Not so in golf. Once the shot is made, there is no do-over. A bad shot that lands in the lake or in the bushes can't be corrected with the next shot. Many choices are like that.

I read about a pharmacist who made a quick choice. A man rushed into a drug store and said to the pharmacist, "Quick! Give me something for the hiccups!" The pharmacist threw a glass of water in his face.

"Why did you do that?"

"You don't have the hiccups now, do you?"

"No, but my wife in the car still does."

It's easy to make big mistakes when making quick choices.

As Christians we must adopt God's principles to live our lives effectively for Jesus, our Lord. Here are a few principles that I have identified:

- God created the universe and all things big and small.
- The Holy Bible is God's inspired work and contains the truth.
- God seeks a personal relationship with me.
- God is divine and I am human.
- I will never understand God.
- I can ask God for direction and advice, and He will give it to me.
- His advice has infinite wisdom, whereas my choices are limited by my knowledge.

Since I accept the worldview that God is my Creator, and if I am going to be an effective Christian, I must align my response to these principles.

A Pharisee asked Jesus a question:

> Teacher, which is the greatest commandment in the Law? Jesus replied, "Love the Lord your God with all your heart and with all your soul and with all your mind." This is the first and greatest commandment. And the second is like it: "Love your neighbor as yourself." All the Law and the Prophets hang on these two commandments. (Matt. 22:36–40)

The apostle Peter spells out the values we should select:

> Make every effort to add to your faith, goodness; and to goodness, knowledge; and to knowledge, self-control; and to self-control, perseverance; and to perseverance, godliness; and to godliness, mutual affection; and to mutual affection, love. For if you possess these qualities in increasing measure, they will keep you from being ineffective and unproductive in your knowledge of our Lord Jesus Christ. But whoever does not have them is nearsighted and blind, forgetting that they have been cleansed from their past sins. (2 Peter 1:5–9)

Life is full of choices, and who we become is a product of those choices. How we make those choices is important. Do we make impulsive choices? Or are our choices well thought out and based on godly principles? Do we stop in the gap between stimulus and response to make our choices based on the above principles and directed by God?

Today was not necessarily a day to shame myself over past bad decisions but a day to honestly reflect on some of my poor choices and determine if there is a pattern. I found there is a clear pattern: The choices I made that have worked well for me have been those made in collaboration with the Lord. Praying and seeking God's guidance has never led me into a bad decision.

The choices that have not worked out well for me have been those made on impulse without consulting the Creator of the universe who is the repository of all wisdom. Choices have not worked out well when I have reacted in anger and not love or was selfish and not selfless.

Good and Bad Choices

In 1991, God infused a mission in me to build a consulting business based upon Christian values. Every morning I prayed for God to fill me up and make me more like Jesus. Even though I depleted all my savings and ran my credit cards to the max, I never once doubted that God would guide me through the mission He gave me. At the end of August 1992, with all savings gone and credit cards maxed out, the business began to turn around. By the end of 1992, my savings were replenished, the cards were paid off, and I had cleared $14,000 profit for the year. Six years after starting The Rainmaker Companies, other consultants were joining me, and business was booming.

But I hired a consultant without taking my choice to the Lord. To not offend people of other faiths, this man persuaded me to remove from our marketing materials the line that said, "We abide by the Christian value of integrity." Within a month, I learned this consultant was working behind my back to leave me and take away my largest client. I lifted the matter to the Lord, and He led me to fire the consultant and return the reference to Christian values to my marketing materials.

A few months later, a potential client told me if I would remove the reference to Christianity, they would hire me. I learned from the previous experience to pray about matters like this. God said, *If you deny me, I will deny you.* I refused to remove the reference, and the potential client hired my competitor.

Within two weeks, a larger prospect hired me. The managing partner said he wanted someone who held Christian values. He told me, "I have partners and employees of other religions, but because you stood for Christian values, you let people know who you are." From that day forward, Rainmaker's references to Christian values permanently remained within its materials.

Around 5:30 that evening, Sheryl drove me back to MM 366, north of Glenrock Branch, and by 7:30, six more miles were completed.

Yesterday morning I was painfully exhausted. It hasn't gotten any worse, and even through the pain, I have been able to cover twenty miles each day. God is with me in this trial, and I am counting it pure joy. Praise God for the superhuman strength He is granting me.

Chapter 26

Joy—Heaven on Earth

Joy does not simply happen to us. We have to choose joy and keep choosing it every day.
—Henri Nouwen

July 30, 2014

WEDNESDAY WAS DAY TWENTY-SIX OF the walk. We left Chunky and Gail's home early this morning and Sheryl drove me to MM 372. At first light we saw four deer grazing on a green carpet of grass. Robins were singing in the treetops, praising the Lord for their provisions, knowing He would supply again today. I was heading home, so my morning was launched amid great hope and fanfare. By 10:00 a.m., the journey had taken on the feel of the demanding last days of a second-rate traveling stage production.

After my morning walk, we were going to drive home to Leiper's Fork, twenty-seven miles from the end of the trace and about thirty-five miles from where I was to end up this morning. The pain in my lower extremities was overwhelming, but as I started moving, the pain began to subside, giving way to thought and prayer. The Lord blessed me with a numbness to the pain at about one mile into my walk.

Ten miles in four and a half hours is my limit this morning. Sheryl has been waiting for me near Jack's Branch and almost to the Meriwether Lewis National Monument. She brought me some cold chocolate milk and Advil. After I sat in the car for the ride home, my joints and muscles began to stiffen. At home, after an hour-long therapeutic swim, I unloaded the Tahoe for what will be this trip's last time. I can see the finish line in my mind, and I am thanking God for seeing us through the walk with no serious calamities.

My friend Jonathan Hughes called me this afternoon to say he is planning to walk with me tomorrow morning. Meeting at 4:30 a.m. is no problem for Jonathan as he is an energetic and positive early bird. Since I arrived at Hillsboro United Methodist Church (UMC) in 2006, Jonathan has been my very special friend. He is the forty-eight-year-old son of Horace and Betty Hughes, whose family members have attended the church since its early days. During the school year Jonathan works with handicapped children and farms the rest of the year. He will normally have forty or fifty goats in his herd.

Of anyone I have ever met, Jonathan is the most truthful. I had been divorced for five years before I met Sheryl. During that time, I brought three different women to visit Hillsboro UMC with me. Jonathan always made it a point to meet and chat with each one. The second time Sheryl came to church with me, he came up to her during our meet and greet and said, "Sheryl, of all the women Troy has brought to this church, you are the cream of the crop." I didn't know what to say, whether I should crawl under a pew or hide my head in shame. But Sheryl felt affirmed. That is just the way Jonathan is; he tells it like he sees it, the truth with no filter.

Today's Reflections

I was very conscious that God was helping me experience true joy in the midst of a major trial of my life. The pain and exhaustion I felt was punctuated minute by minute by the pure joy of the power of God moving through my body and soul. During my quiet time this morning, the Holy Spirit encouraged me to reflect on joy today. On such a beautiful and invigorating morning, it seems a fitting prayer focus.

What is joy? Is it happiness? Is it bliss? Have I experienced it? Can we have it while we are on this earth?

In the movie *The Bucket List*, Morgan Freeman's character asks the Jack Nicholson character, "What has brought you joy?" Nicholson was stumped by the question. He had lived a productive life, enjoyed monetary successes, and faced several divorces and broken relationships, but he couldn't answer the question. When I saw that movie, I felt an emptiness because it was difficult for me to point to any sustained period of joy in my own life.

Joy is not a normal occurrence; it has been rare for me. I haven't been able to craft it in my workshop or create it through an experience of hard work or pleasure. I haven't found joy in happiness, pleasure, or good times.

Joy is something I have experienced through a divine, supernatural relationship with God working in other people. Even when joy occurs infrequently, we remember the sacred feelings.

Trials and overwhelming difficulties come to everyone—they are a part of life. Christians fail in business, have heart attacks, get fired, get rejected, and have accidents. They experience the same things that those who don't know Him experience.

I have to ask myself how many times have trials and troubles produced joy during the time of the trial? This walk is a trial, but I have been joyful every day. Through the pain of this 444-mile walk, I am realizing joy is connected to my pain. This day I choose to be joyful as I am overwhelmed with gratitude.

Periodically we help serve lunch to the poor and homeless guests at Community Care Fellowship. Normally about one hundred men, women, and children enjoy a well-prepared meal in a warm and safe environment. One Friday, Keith Elder and James Dean Hicks helped serve lunch. Keith brought a guitar to provide a little entertainment. Lunch at CCF is a bit chaotic, with people being paged for the shower or their laundry. It took several minutes for the crowd to settle down as Keith began playing and singing.

One of the guests asked James if he knew the song "Three Wooden Crosses." As James began to strum the tune, a homeless man began singing the song in a most beautiful voice. Several others joined in the singing, some harmonizing. There were tears of joy and gratitude. In the midst of extreme poverty and homelessness, men and women felt the presence of God through the medium of music. Whenever I recall that day, joy floods my soul.

Troy Waugh

Happiness Is Not Joy

People get overly excited about sports. When the Tennessee Titans went to the Super Bowl and the Predators played for the Stanley cup, fans all over the state went wild. Around the world people worship their sports and their teams. People enjoy watching games, kicking balls, hitting them, and running with balls, including little children and big fat men. This is fun and happiness but not joy.

One of my mother's favorite verses was James 1:2: "Consider it pure joy my brothers and sisters, when you face trials of many kinds." I read this Scripture at her funeral and talked about the many trials she endured during her lifetime. Many of those trials she never talked about to me, but some were revealed in hushed tones by family members in the years following her death. She was certainly a tortured soul on this earth, but I know she has found peace and joy in heaven.

Only in recent years have I come to grasp some of the meaning in the James verses. Most times, when a difficult period or trial has been dealt me, I couldn't see God's hand in it during the trial, and I found no joy. Years or months later, I could look back and see the Lord shepherding me through the difficulty and teaching me a lesson. It was during the trials that I matured and learned to grapple with difficult situations and gained experience necessary to meet life head on.

As I have grown in my faith, I have learned to seek the joy while the trial is underway.

Corrie Ten Boom wrote, "Every experience God gives us, every person He puts in our lives is the perfect preparation for the future that only He can see." You could replace the word *experience* with the word *trial*.

This became true for me in 1991 when God opened up a new career for me. The desire of my heart had always been to be successful in business. For almost thirty years, I could not gain any business momentum. My life had been one or two years here and one or two years there, moving around the country, changing jobs, changing focus, and changing relationships.

In April 1991, I felt the overwhelming presence of the Holy Spirit, Who spoke clearly to me. He instructed me to return to the accounting profession and help accountants build their businesses. The following twenty-three years from launch to sale provided a very satisfying business career.

However, the joy of building my earthly heart's desire has been overshadowed by the joy of learning to live more fully in the arms of Jesus through peace and turmoil.

Finding Joy

True joy makes life worth living. The Bible tells us we can choose joy. I have experienced being part of the same event with another person, yet may have a completely different appreciation for it. One person could be happy and choose joy, while the other may choose despair and be destroyed by it.

Sheryl and I have two friends who are in their nineties. Bob and Emmie Cummings lived in our community for many years, but now Bob lives in an assisted-living apartment, and Emmie lives in a secure memory-care unit. While we were visiting Bob and Emmie, Sheryl noticed that Emmie needed a hair trim. When she asked Emmie if she'd like one, her face lit up and she said, "Oh yes!"

Sheryl didn't have her equipment for trimming Emmie's hair, so we came back a few days later. When we returned, Bob was not with Emmie, and she became very agitated and seemed afraid of us. She didn't respond to Sheryl or allow herself to be touched.

During a very difficult fifteen minutes or so we tried to communicate. Just then Bob walked through the door. While Emmie's memory seemed blank, her feelings had memories of the joy Bob brought her. Her face shone with the biggest smile you have ever seen. Her body and persona relaxed, her agitation disappeared, and her entire being radiated her joy of being with Bob.

After a few minutes, Bob helped Emmie sit so Sheryl could trim and style her hair. Bob sat beside her, and she remained relaxed for the entire session. We both experienced pure joy as we watched Bob feed her lunch and talk with her. Our hearts stayed full the rest of that splendid day and infuses us with joy every time we recall it.

Joy on earth comes from realizing God is doing something splendid in and around us.

His Ways Are Not Our Ways

Living the Christian life in joy requires a completely different approach. Scripture teaches us the rich will be poor and the poor will be rich. The strong will be weak and the weak will be strong. And there will be pure joy in trials.

Joy is sometimes concealed in kindness. Kindness often requires empathy and may require me to suffer with another human. Being with, offering my presence to another person in the midst of his trials, can bring me immeasurable joy. This is more than the happiness of winning a ball game or the excitement brought by a good golf shot. Simply being present for a friend in trouble, in his pain and brokenness, and in the sharing of our humanness can bring us the most profound joy.

Trials and Joy Come Together

The apostle James seems to say that joy and trials always come together. Only in recent years have I been able to realize this wonderful and amazing phenomenon. When I have been overwhelmed with trouble or grief, I've learned that a true friend can bring joy into my life. Avoiding trials does not bring joy. It seems I cannot experience joy without trouble or trials. Trials are required for my spiritual growth.

Through this walk, I have found a more encompassing joy—a joy springing up from the remarkable capacity God is infusing within me. Repenting again and again, daily and hourly, and accepting the forgiveness for my awful sins has produced a height of joy for me. I have gone from feeling and believing I was powerless a few months ago to depending on the limitless love of God.

The apostle John quoted Jesus, "Very truly, I tell you, my Father will give you whatever you ask in my name. Until now you have not asked for anything in my name. Ask and you will receive, and your joy will be complete" (John 16:23–24).

At times, I can't feel joy or see it, especially when it hurts. However, as my faith has grown, I am learning to experience joy in the midst of trials.

I've learned that what brings me true joy is not business success but abiding in Jesus right here, day by day, on this walk on the Natchez Trace. I have found serene *joy*—divine delight and total satisfaction resting in the arms of Jesus. I am totally weakened physically, but the power of God flowing through me today creates an unbelievable strength that I've never known before. Realizing that the power of God flows through me brings me pure joy.

Late in the afternoon, we returned to MM 382, and we walked two hours, covering five miles.

After our walk, we drove back to MM 384 to visit the gravesite of Meriwether Lewis of Lewis and Clark expedition fame. He died mysteriously here on the trace, but no one knows if it was murder or suicide.

Nearly two centuries after the event, we may never discover exactly what happened that night along the Natchez Trace when one of the nation's greatest heroes died at the tragically young age of thirty-five.

My pace has really slowed to below three miles an hour. It's just a function of the pain and stiffness in my muscles and joints. A few more days and I may be crawling. Praise God, tonight I get to spend the night in my own bed.

Chapter 27

Discipleship and Leadership

Don't wish it was easier; wish that you were better. Don't wish for less problems; wish for more skills. Don't wish for less challenges; wish for more wisdom.
—Jim Rohn

July 31, 2014

ON THURSDAY MORNING, THE TWENTY-SEVENTH day of my walk, Jonathan Hughes met me at 4:30 a.m. at the Garrison Creek rest area. He drove his truck to a rest area near our target for the day—MM 401—and parked it there. I appreciated Jonathan for giving Sheryl some relief. Then he jumped in my Tahoe, and we parked it at the starting point, MM 387. After walking the fourteen miles by 10:30, we rode in his truck back to mine at the starting point.

Today's Reflections

That morning I got up especially early to have my quiet time with the Lord. I heard the words, *You are becoming my disciple, but I want you to be a follower, not a leader.* That seemed like an odd message, so I was looking forward to my prayers and reflections on the road. As I walked today, the Holy Spirit gave me a new perspective on how discipleship and leadership fit together.

Many years passed before I felt satisfied with my Christian walk.

Yes, I had been saved. My ticket to heaven was punched. I believed the Lord died for my eternal salvation. Yet I viewed my salvation almost like a pass-fail class I took in college fifty years ago. I did just enough to pass the course back then, but I hadn't grown in the subject since.

Until I was fifty years old, I could not point to one single person whom I had led to the Lord. I didn't know anyone on whom I'd had a positive Christian influence. I may have had some lasting impact on my children; however, there were equal amounts of negative influence. I had borne very little fruit, and that was sad.

It was encouraging when Jonathan told me I had been a good Christian influence on him since we met over twelve years earlier. He told me I reminded him of his own father, who passed away a few years ago.

Go Make Disciples

It has only been in more recent years that I have come to understand the meaning of Jesus's final commandment in Matthew 28:18–19:

> Then Jesus came to them and said, "All authority in heaven and on earth has been given to me. Therefore, go and make disciples of all nations, baptizing them in the name of the Father and of the Son and of the Holy Spirit."

Accepting Jesus as my Savior was one step toward a new life in Christ, a transformed life of sanctification and joy on this earth. It was also a step toward a life so passionate about my love for Jesus that I could be a disciple and a positive influence on those around me. But I was stuck on that step for way too many years.

Growing in my faith and in my discipleship does not make me a super-Christian. It does make me more aware of my own inadequacies and my need for God. My personal faith will grow through discipleship development and may also influence other people to do the same. Or it may cause others to see my sinful self and my inadequacies and know what a hypocrite I really am.

Followers Make Good Leaders

The great leaders in the Bible were prepared and powered by God for discipling others. Based on Moses's seventy elders, the example was

Discipleship and Leadership

set for the twelve disciples to lead others. Moses's elders and Jesus's disciples called on the divine power of God to lead.

Like many of the opposites in our spiritual lives, we must first be good followers to be leaders for Jesus. There is something attractive and contagious about a total dedication to living one's life for Jesus that points people to Jesus. The moment I begin trying to lead people to me is the moment I repel them and destroy my witness for God.

Through my participation in the All-In program of Christian Leadership Concepts, I have learned there are several ingredients that go into making a disciple.

Self-Knowledge

The most magnetic disciples and the greatest leaders understand themselves. Rather than operating on impulse, the best disciples seek to understand their own motivations. I've found men and women who have the most self-knowledge, who understand what makes them sin and what makes them walk with the Lord, will usually be the most effective disciple-makers.

Trustworthiness

When people trust you, they are more likely to follow you. People will trust you more if they know your intent is in their best interests. Some Christians speak one way and act another. When you do what you say you will do, and your words and actions are aligned, and you keep your promises, followers see.

Preparation

Great disciples and leaders practice the disciplines of reading Scripture, praying diligently, and preparing for that moment when God opens a door for them to witness.

Critical Prayer and Thinking

Leaders invest time in praying about their plans and relationships. Praying reveals God's plans for the leader. The ability to align one's plans with God's plans is a force multiplier in any endeavor. The apostle Peter tells us in 2 Peter 1:3, "His divine power has given us everything we need for a godly life." Only in recent years have I begun to pray with and for my clients.

Self-Discipline

The discipline to study, to follow through on promises, to prepare for witness opportunities, and to pray are all important ingredients to being effective and productive. Peter goes on to say, "For this very reason, make every effort to add to your faith goodness; and to goodness, knowledge; and to knowledge, self-control" (2 Peter 1:5–6). In this world of distractions, it is easy to get sidetracked by meaningless activity. I have learned that if Satan cannot make a leader a bad sinner, he will tempt us to be busy doing good things that are not aligned with God's purposes. By distracting us, Satan sabotages God's plans, making us less effective.

For much of my life, I have distorted the meaning of the gospel. Satisfied my ticket to heaven was punched, I succumbed to the consumer-oriented, entertainment-providing, forgiveness-only gospel. Forgiveness-only and grace-only is only part of the truth. With this kind of gospel, I could go right on with self-centered, intentional sinning.

There are many adherents to the prosperity gospel, a gospel that turns people into consumers of religious entertainment and the positive-thinking and transactional aspects of the kingdom. Both the forgiveness-only gospel and the prosperity gospel make no room for the ways and means that Jesus passed on to his followers. Neither has a serious connection to character transformation, and neither expects everyone who is "saved" to actually follow Jesus.

Moreover, these gospels don't set the precedent for making disciple-leaders who make disciples. Both of these gospels separate conversion from discipleship. In this tradition, real discipleship is optional and transformation is stunted. It seems one can't make a Christlike disciple from a non-discipleship gospel.

A False Gospel

A partial gospel is a false gospel. A partial gospel teaches everyone is a Christian who agrees that Jesus died for his sins, rose from the dead, ascended into heaven, and will return someday to gather His church. By the way, you don't need to do anything about it; in fact, you *can't* do anything about it because it is all by grace.

While these tenets of the faith are all true, this gospel is incomplete.

I never realized that making and multiplying disciples was expected of me, so I didn't do that until the last twenty-five years of my life.

The ways and means that Jesus prescribed have not changed.

Non-discipleship gospels are advanced through many powerful forms of media, but they won't multiply through transformed lives of disciples who are making still more disciples. They can't. People with discipleship DNA are still needed for reproduction and multiplication. They are a must, no substitutes. Converts galore will never accomplish what a few sold-out, committed disciples can do for the kingdom of God.

~~~

Jonathan Hughes, who walked with me today, is a disciple of the Lord who influences many other people with his friendship and love. Whenever Jonathan has attended a Titans football game with me, he has gathered forty or fifty coupon booklets from the cup holders on each seat. The following week, he takes these coupon booklets to his friends. Each of his friends is delighted when Jonathan shows up with his smiling face and a gift. A giving person, he regularly shows up at our house with a gift. He has brought us a burn barrel, a beautiful, artful tree branch, a metal sculpture, and a night light. Jonathan exemplifies sharing the love of Christ with his neighbors.

~~~

Based on my experience of leading work teams and discipling mission teams, NFP organizations and individuals, I have found five major elements to good discipleship and leadership.

1. Self-Discipleship and Leadership

An enthusiastic disciple of the Lord will attract others. When a follower exhibits personal disciplines, others develop their own faith. Before anyone will follow you, you must prove yourself to be a person worthy of followers. If your personal habits are poor, your relationship with the Lord cursory, and your direction aimless, people will not be attracted to your leadership. Self-discipleship is a prerequisite for discipling anyone else.

2. Team-Discipleship and Leadership

When a team of disciples works together, great things happen for the Lord and for the salvation of others.

John Wesley believed in the use of small groups to build disciples. He felt too many people can hide in the megachurches, where there is little accountability. Small groups like our Praying Men and CLC and our discipleship classes offer ways to grow and disciple each other.

In his book *The 21 Irrefutable Laws of Leadership: Follow Them and People Will Follow You*, John Maxwell says we have a choice of either addition or multiplication. We can disciple people and help them be successful, or we can raise up leaders who will disciple other disciples.

3. A Compelling Mission

Jesus said, "Therefore go and make disciples of all nations, baptizing them in the name of the Father and of the Son and of the Holy Spirit, and teaching them to obey everything I have commanded you. And surely I am with you always, to the very end of the age" (Matt. 28:19–20).

This is called the Great Commission, and it is the most powerful mission ever with a huge purpose, beyond what any one human being can do.

A leader with a compelling mission can influence people far beyond his or her lifetime and influence a new cadre of leaders that cascades down the decades. Some of the greatest leaders are people who never held office: Jesus, Mother Teresa, and Martin Luther King Jr. Their compelling missions and influence have changed the world for the better.

4. Influence

John Maxwell defines leadership as influence—nothing more, nothing less. People with the most influence lead from who they are and how they interact with others. Disciples and leaders who are passionate about their mission attract others who want to be part of a team with purpose. A respected self-leader with passion for a mission will inspire others to join his team.

5. Perspective

One of the crucial understandings that everyone must have when discipling others is that everyone has a different perspective. Every person you disciple has different family experiences, education, and communication styles. Because of these and many other differences, you cannot take a one-size-fits-all approach to discipling.

During the early evening portion of the walk, after completing six more miles, Jonathan and I stopped at MM 405 to view Jackson Falls, which was named after President Andrew Jackson. He used the trace to march his soldiers to and from the Battle of New Orleans. We ended our day at MM 407.

Chapter 28

Selective Sins

Christians can be selective as to which sins they hate. Many of the same Christians who hotly condemn homosexuality, which Jesus never mentioned, disregard His straightforward commands against divorce, lust, and pride.
—Philip Yancey

August 1, 2014

ON FRIDAY, DAY TWENTY-EIGHT OF the walk, Jonathan met me at MM 418 where we left his truck. Then we traveled to our starting point for the day at MM 407. While my body ached, Jonathan cheered me up with his enthusiasm for life. We covered eleven miles, and he wasn't even tired. Today is my seventieth birthday and was the original target date for the completion of this 444-mile journey, but we still have twenty-four miles to go.

At MM 408, we stopped briefly to visit the Gordon House and ferry site. This is one of two Old Natchez Trace structures still standing. The Gordon House is over two hundred years old and was the home of John and Dolly Gordon, who ran the ferry across the Duck River. Dolly managed a 1,500-acre plantation, raised ten children, and lived here forty years after John died. The National Park Service has plans to make it an interpretive center.

Troy Waugh

Today's Reflections

This morning the Holy Spirit urged me to reflect on sin. As we walked, Jonathan and I had great conversation about heaven, hell, and sin, and prayed together. When Jonathan prays, he prays for many other people and their needs. He is not self-centered and is truly concerned about the lives of other people. He just loves to do things for other people.

"What do you think sin is?" I asked Jonathan.

He said, "Sin is doing something bad that God doesn't want you to do, or it's not doing something good that you should do."

I think he captured it accurately.

I've observed that serious discussions can get real ugly, real fast, in person or on Twitter or Facebook. Wherever people, Christians or non-Christians, communicate on religion, government, politics, faith, life, sex, race, love, etc., it isn't long before comments can get hostile, voices are raised, names called, motives impugned, and self-appointed sin cops draw their Tasers and start frying people.

As an aside, have you heard the one about YouTube, Twitter, and Facebook merging? They will call the merged company You Twit Face.

Most hostility derives from a belief that another person's sin is worth more condemnation than mine. It is so easy to slip into the role of a modern-day Pharisee and become delusional and blind to one's own violations of God's Law.

One of the key reasons for me doing this walk is to avoid smuggling the sins of my past into my future. Many folks don't like to admit this, but sins are embedded in us by nature. Adam and Eve were warned to stay away from the Tree of the Knowledge of Good and Evil. God provided an abundance of food all around the Garden of Eden, but they were not allowed to eat of that one. Just think, only one sin.

The word *sin* essentially means to "miss the mark." It's the way the Bible describes a life that doesn't measure up to God's standard. Like Jonathan says, sin can be intentional or sin can be an omission, "Not doing something I should do." When we sin, we are separated from God.

When I became a Christian, I foolishly expected all my sins and temptations would magically disappear, and my evil desires and selfish impulses would suddenly be no more. I thought at the moment of my conversion that I would be transformed and no longer sin against God.

Needless to say, that did not happen. For some reason, I still became violently angry and verbally and physically abusive. My greed seemed to infect me to the core, and I made impulsive decisions based on lust, money, and power.

Beginning at about age thirteen, with hormones raging, lust for women seemed to dominate my thinking. I began acting it out wherever and whenever I had a willing partner. In those days, internet pornography hadn't been invented, but lusty magazines were available. Finding provocative magazines in the homes of relatives or friends cultivated my ideation of sexual exploits.

I have learned that a sinful imagination can be a powerful force that separates us from God. When we focus on the glitter of this world, we are not focused on God. When we are separated from God, we are sinning.

The Discipleship Process

Only in the last twenty years have I come to understand how conversion, discipleship, and sanctification seem to work. Discipleship is a journey from conversion to sanctification. Yes, on the day we confess our belief in the Lord Jesus Christ, we are transformed from death to eternal life. However, sin still infects our human body.

For example, one day a person could be an unsaved drunk. The moment he turns his life over to Jesus, he becomes a saved drunk. And although saved, he is still a sinful drunk. From that point forward, step by step, he must die to his worldly desires. The spiritual growth that takes place in a person is a journey; the length of that journey is different for everyone.

This walk is another opportunity to turn my sinful nature over to the healing power of God.

Some start immediately on the journey and begin to eradicate the intentional sins in their lives. At my young and naïve age, I thought, *Hey, I'm going to heaven. I'm having too much fun to give up these desires.* Satan was trying to take me back.

Six Hundred, Ten, and Two

The old Jewish Law counted over six hundred sins. God determined the people couldn't abide by those, so He gave Moses a list of ten commandments. Humans continued to sin. God sent Jesus, as atonement for our sins, and he took on the penalty for our sins. Jesus left us with two commandments: Love God with all your heart, and love your neighbor as yourself. Jesus said all the Law hangs on these two commandments.

Sugarcoated Sin

For many years, I rationalized my behavior and failed to come to terms with my own sins. I glossed over my own sins and condemned the sins of others. I sugarcoated my greed by saying, "That's just the way the business world works." I spent a huge amount of my time and energy chasing the dollar and ignoring the commandments to love God and my neighbor. Worst of all, I damaged my family, harmed other people, and lived as a hypocritical example of a Christian. I became the slave of my desires, yet piously condemned others over their choice of sin.

When we make someone else feel bad about what they're doing and who they are, and we shame them, we are not exhibiting love. This is sick, twisted, and evil. I have encountered Christians who use the verses of the Bible, especially in the Old Testament, as knives to carve others into the Christians they think they should be.

Two men whom I thought were my friends and good Christians told me I wasn't qualified to lead a men's discipleship group because I wouldn't call a certain group a cult. I told them, "These people do some strange things, things that don't seem Christian to me, but I'm not into name calling and judging. If someone tells me he or she has accepted Jesus as his personal Savior, I accept that. That is for them to take to the Lord."

These well-meaning brothers seemed to be saying, *Oh here, allow me to pull a sharp knife out of the drawer and cut that out of you.* Or, *Look at me, I'm a better Christian than you are because I pointed out your sin and fixed you.* These friends couched their comments as correction. I felt judged and didn't sense Jesus anywhere in the conversation.

The sin cops (modern-day Pharisees) arrive thumping their Bibles, ready to throw us into prison while they guard the gates of heaven. It is as if they are piously proclaiming, *Shame on you. Look at me. I have the Law right here. You are my inferior.* They unleash the "Lord's fury" in sanctimonious terms without regard to loving God or of loving others.

God granted us free will to make choices. If an adulterer doesn't steal, will it make him a better man and vice versa? A drunkard may not be an adulterer, but he defiles his body with poison. I have been amused watching a three hundred-pound preacher rail against alcohol use or smoking.

Sin Divides

Non-Christians laugh at those of us who split with our Christian brothers over man-made or interpreted Scripture. *I'm not going to accept you because you aren't baptized.* Or, *You're not a Christian because you don't accept the Baptist (or Presbyterian or Methodist) doctrine.* Or, *Christians don't allow pianos in their churches.* On and on it goes as Christians fight each other and Satan laughs.

In the biblical story of the woman who was caught in the act of adultery, John shows us we are all sinful human beings whose insecurities can tug us in all sorts of wrong directions (John 8:2–11). The woman was publicly shamed, humiliated, and about to be stoned by accusers who sought to hide behind a facade of religious superiority.

Yes, this woman sinned; she missed the mark, and she was regretful. The Pharisees were also sinners with their pride and arrogance, even though they appeared more respectable.

We often wear masks to hide our own sins. Some people sin in public; others sin by feeling superior to such people. Either way, we miss the mark; we are separated from God and not following Jesus's most important two commandments. God is most concerned about our hearts, inside our souls.

Christian denominations have been divided into countless splintered groups and subgroups over which selected sins are acceptable and which interpretations of Scripture are correct. Without the power of the Holy Spirit and our own restraint, we tend to interpret the Law as it suits us and condemn others' interpretations. Jesus speaks on this very subject:

> Do not judge, or you too will be judged. For in the same way you judge others, you will be judged, and with the measure you use, it will be measured to you. Why do you look at the speck of sawdust in your brother's eye and pay no attention to the plank in your own eye? How can you say to your brother, "Let me take the speck out of your eye," when all the time there is a plank in your own eye? You hypocrite,

> first take the plank out of your own eye, and then you will
> see clearly to remove the speck from your brother's eye.
> (Matt. 7:1–6)

Modern-day Pharisees infect churches, Facebook, sermons, and radio talk shows, seeking out any hint of sin. Good Christians shoot the wounded and kill hearts and souls, all in the name of the Lord. I do not want to be a Pharisee, whose judgment is visible and whose condemnation brings death.

Lord, forgive my sins, especially when I've judged others.

Sheryl had planned a quiet birthday celebration for me tonight at one of my favorite Italian restaurants, Buca di Beppo. I thought there would be just four of us, but all Sheryl's stepdaughters came, Robin, Carla, and Kim. My son Brian joined us. Also, Leanna, Jason, and Daniel came, along with our friends Buster and Darlene. Carla and Kim's daughters, Mattie, Carly, and Ally joined us. We had a grand time enjoying a robust Italian dinner with an amazing chocolate dessert.

While I enjoyed the love of my family and friends, I felt physically and emotionally drained that night. Was exhaustion to be the symbol for the milestone of my seventieth birthday? Had God emptied me in every way possible to fill me again, beginning tomorrow?

That night my dreams were disjointed. I saw my father's ink- and tobacco-stained hand. I felt my mother's fingers in my hair. I walked through the house in which I grew up one more time, visited the basement of regrets, smelled the apple pie in the oven, looked out the picture window of distant dreams, and wrestled with the choices of my life. I played in the yard, chased the squirrels and rabbits, threw the ball to my English shepherd, and collected the fireflies of days gone by.

Today was the day I was to reach the goal of 444 miles, the end of the trace, and celebrate at the Loveless Café in Nashville. I hadn't quite made it, but I realized true joy comes from the reaching and the striving for a goal.

My goal had been to walk the trace with Jesus. The attainment of a goal is momentary. I would experience that in a few days. Right now, I was determined to savor this communion with my Lord and this walk into new corridors of a new heart.

Chapter 29

Correction and Judgment

Who was I to judge the heart which broke into that moment, spilling kindness and longing? Who was I to dismiss her story because I did not know it?
—Edwina Gateley, *Soul Sisters: Women in Scripture Speak to Women Today*

August 2, 2014

SATURDAY WAS THE TWENTY-NINTH DAY of the walk. While yesterday was my original completion goal, I had pushed as hard as possible, but there are still sixteen miles to go.

Today we have a different troop of four. My sister, Alice Waugh, and her best friend who is like a sister to her, Martha Greene, came to walk with me this morning. Jonathan also joined us, so we had a merry band.

Every morning a new world is created. There are never two days alike. Beginning at MM 428, north of the Gordon House, we started about 6:00 a.m. The orange rays of the sun poked through the remnants of the night, making us all happy to experience being together in nature. We walked till 10:40, covering ten miles.

Troy Waugh

Today's Reflections

This morning, the Holy Spirit seemed to urge me to reflect on correction and judgment, a subject I have been thinking about lately.

On our walk today, Martha and Jonathan had a particularly robust conversation about being judged. Neither of them liked the feeling they got when their motives or actions were judged by other Christians.

While the Bible exhorts us to teach and correct our brethren, Jesus also teaches not to judge. I have found when I attempt to correct someone and he feels judged, he does not listen. In fact, he may defensively adhere to his position more vigorously. That seems to be human nature.

How should we then teach or correct someone? How should we receive correction? How can we correct without judging? Or more importantly, how can we correct without the other person feeling judged?

Johnny was one of my shipmates in Barcelona, Spain, in 1964. He professed a strong Christian belief and belonged to a strict, legalistic denomination that banned musical instruments from their worship. Although I had been a Christian for twelve years, I had not grown in my faith. Johnny believed solely in the New Testament, that one must be baptized to be saved, that regular church attendance was required, and that we get to heaven based upon our own works. He believed people who did not belong to his church were not saved.

My father had grown up in that denomination, and his mother told him when he started going to the Baptist church with my mother, "Now that you are not a member of our church, I don't expect to see you in heaven."

At various times, Johnny and I would have religious conversations. His mission was to convert me to his way of thinking and worshiping. One night, we had been ashore late into the night and both had been drinking some of the local brew. I asked Johnny, "You don't allow pianos in your church; why do you allow toilets? They are not mentioned in the New Testament." Johnny blew up in anger and kicked me—a memorable kick from my long-legged friend. When I punched a small, sarcastic hole in his belief, he could not tolerate such heresy. Uncharacteristically, I did not kick back. Johnny was bigger and also outranked me.

In all our conversations, Johnny claimed he was correcting me; however, I felt he was judging me. He was not only judging, he was kicking me!

Godly Correction

I enjoy robust conversations about religion, politics, sports, and raising children. However, once I feel I am being judged, I struggle to maintain my composure. When the name calling starts, the conversation moves from conflict to hostility.

Greg and Shelvi Gilmore are friends who've worked twenty-four years on foreign mission fields. They've encountered people of all faiths and belief systems and those with no faith in God. Greg said in talking with someone of another faith, or an atheist, if he begins the conversation by criticizing the other person's belief system, that person becomes defensive and shuts down the conversation. He told me he had to earn the right to speak into another person's life. He needed to carry out the most important commands of Jesus—loving God with all your heart and loving your neighbor as yourself. Greg said the Holy Spirit would guide him with the proper timing and the proper words. He learned if he loved the men and women he was ministering to and they sensed that love, they would be open to learning about the one true God.

Francis Chan, a modern theologian and teacher, said about discussing a particular sin, "I don't begin with the sin. That is the wrong place. I take someone to the Scripture and we read it together." The Bible does not say we are to correct someone else; it is the Scripture that is useful for correcting. "All Scripture is God-breathed and is useful for teaching, rebuking, correcting and training in righteousness" (2 Tim. 3:16).

Many people seem to have an entrenched belief system called confirmation bias. That means that we believe something emotionally, sometimes irrationally, then look for facts to back up our emotional point of view. This emotional belief becomes so entrenched in our psyche that we have little tolerance for disagreement.

Yes, godly correction is allowed and may be necessary. Yet for the receiver of correction, there is a huge danger of feeling judged. So should we shy away from correction?

Demonstrating Love

Greg and Shelvi learned in their mission work to offer many occasions of hospitality, friendship, and love before engaging people in a conversation about God. In many cases, the nonbeliever would bring it up. Greg and Shelvi would demonstrate their love, and that example would speak for itself.

Strangers are often violently opposed to correction and teaching, whereas friends may be more eager to learn.

A couple was eating breakfast one morning when they saw the neighbor hanging out the laundry. The woman said, "That laundry doesn't look clean!"

The man responded, "Maybe she doesn't know how to wash clothes, or she needs a better laundry detergent."

They noticed the dingy laundry each time the dirty-looking laundry was hung out and always remarked about it.

One day, they saw the neighbor hang up clean laundry. Then they remembered they had washed their windows the day before. They had been viewing clean laundry through dirty windows.

In Matthew 7:5, Jesus doesn't say it is inappropriate to address a speck in our brother's eye. The couple observing the dirty laundry were being self-righteous; they needed to remove the specks on their own windows.

There is no justification for wounding a nonbeliever or a fellow Christian with judgmental words. We often hear Christians have a tendency to shoot their wounded.

That's like the two hunters in the woods. One of them collapses and stops breathing. The other guy whips out his cell phone and calls 911, telling the operator, "I think my friend is dead. What can I do?"

The operator said, "I can help. First let's make sure he's dead."

There's a silence, then a shot was heard. The guy came back on the phone and says, "Okay, what now?"

Receiving Correction

While teaching and correcting require patience, skill, and the Scripture, receiving the correction calls for even greater openness and restraint. We live in a culture where friends are often afraid to tell the truth because others may charge, You are judging me.

For years, I viewed feedback, teaching, or correction as negative and often became defensive and combative. With a counselor, I worked on changing my willingness to receive feedback. Why was it I could receive correction from my golf coach but became defensive about my Christian beliefs? I had to learn accepting correction and teaching is for our improvement. If I can listen to correction, then I can change and be a better, more dedicated Christian.

A few years ago, I facilitated an all-day training in Cincinnati for about thirty people and felt the day had gone fairly well. As is my custom, at the end of class I asked for feedback on how I could improve. On the plane home I read through the evaluations, which had mostly high marks. Then I came to one that was unsigned but had "lunch" as the response to the question "What was the best part of the day?"

That comment pierced my heart, flattened my spirit, and ruined my trip back home. For several days I fretted and stewed over the jerk who had written it. And still after more than twenty years, that comment sticks in my craw.

Effective Correction

Judgment focuses on shame and makes me feel like a bad person. Effective correction and feedback challenges me to grow into my potential. Judgment tells me I am what I've done in the past, especially the bad things. Judgment tells me I can't grow out of that label and that I may be labeled with the very worst I have done forever. If I explode with anger, judgment tells me I am a murderer. If I am tempted with lust or pornography, judgment tells me I am an adulterer. If I lie, judgment tells me that I am damned to everlasting hell.

The truth of God's Word is radically different. God's Word says I am valuable, I am a child of God, I am an adopted son, and I am an heir to the kingdom. God labels me with His truth.

I have a very small group of friends whom I trust enough to ask for feedback and their advice for my life. To take correction properly, I have to trust that the person giving advice or correction is doing so for my best interests, not just his need to feel superior. When someone corrects me and has not established this trust, my confirmation bias will naturally kick in and cause me to be defensive.

Just because I perceive something as negative doesn't mean that others are being judgmental. It is extremely hard to set aside my entrenched ideas and receive correction without feeling judged.

We cannot get too much good discipleship training and accountability.

Solomon wrote in Proverbs 12:1, "Whoever loves discipline loves knowledge, but whoever hates correction is stupid." Once a person has accepted a lie, growing into the ability to accept correction requires patience, openness, and a willingness to understand.

Giving and receiving correction is a skill and takes a high level of discernment. I have found I must ask permission first before giving advice—even to a friend. I may say, "I may very well be wrong, but this is my observation." I must be humble in the words I use. If possible, I need to reference applicable Scripture. And most of all, I must not call the other person names or impugn his motives.

Harmful Correction

An acquaintance told me, "Your humor is edgy and not acceptable in the kingdom of God." He went on to say, "Your salvation is in jeopardy, and you will be punished. You are not qualified to be an usher, teach a Sunday school class, or lead anything in the church until you clean up your act."

That correction was very harsh and hurtful; I felt humiliated and shamed. I considered his comments carefully, prayed, and did my best not to take them as insults and become angry at him. But this guy had never shown initiative in building a relationship with me. He didn't show any concern for my needs. I concluded that effective correction comes with relationship.

When I don't feel a person has earned the right to correct me, I do my dead level best to not become defensive. I then ask myself some questions: *Do I feel bad because she was right, or was she just being ill mannered? Am I rebelling because of confirmation bias, or does this person have something I should consider?*

A mentor friend can offer correction without the receiver feeling judged. Think of a relationship as a bank account—you make deposits and withdrawals. If you have made significant deposits, you can make withdrawals. If the relationship is long and strong, you have more to work with than with a new friend. Long relationships can withstand the tension of correction.

Be wise in what you say, but don't hold back telling truth in love. Consider the feelings of the other person, but thicken your own skin as well. Perhaps most importantly, keep quiet for a while; you may find your words aren't necessary.

Giving and receiving advice, teaching or correcting, requires extraordinary patience, humility, wisdom, and a relationship of friendship and respect. The giver must realize unsolicited advice may be met with defensiveness. Most of all, the giver must seek the guidance of the Holy Spirit or be prepared for the interaction to go terribly wrong.

After the morning walk, I swam in the pool and rested most of the day. I cannot recall when I have been this physically exhausted. And I know God will pull, push, encourage, and love me through to the end. Sitting in my easy chair, body limp and spent, glazed eyes fixed on nothing, my mind wrapped around two polar opposites: joy and pain. Joy that God has led me into the safe place of trusting Him; pain in every nook of my body.

Chapter 30

Who Is Jesus?

Jesus didn't say, "Blessed are those who care for the poor." He said, "Blessed are we where we are poor, where we are broken." It is there that God loves us deeply and pulls us into deeper communion with Himself.
—Henri Nouwen

August 3, 2014

I AWOKE ON THE MORNING of day thirty with gladness for the conversation I'd been having in my soul. I thought about how I didn't know what would happen when my walk would finally come to an end.

At 6:00 a.m., my trusted friend Jonathan joined me. We dropped his truck at the Garrison Creek rest stop and began at MM 428. A few miles into our walk, Ron and Carol Johnston and John Drueke joined us. It was so wonderful to have friends walk with me. We stopped about 9:00 a.m. so we could get to church on time.

During the service, Pastor Betty announced that anyone wanting to walk with me could meet me this evening at 5:00 to walk across the Natchez Trace Bridge, then again on Monday to walk the last six miles before celebrating with dinner at Loveless Café.

Troy Waugh

Today's Reflections

Today, as on most other days, I was communing with my Lord Jesus.

This morning, the Lord reminded me that He is divine and I am human. I will never fully understand God. However, since He is divine, He understands me. Today I will reflect on this and either get my head around it or resolve to let it go.

Jesus was fully human and is fully God. He was the direct extension of God to the people on this earth. In Him I have placed my trust. Since the day I accepted Christ in 1952, John 3:16 has sustained me. It says, "For God so loved the world that he gave his one and only Son, that whoever believes in him shall not perish but have eternal life."

There are many dimensions to what Jesus did for us when He died on the cross. He took the punishment for our sins. He also provided deliverance from the guilt and shame of those sins. I rely on Paul's words in Romans 8:1: "Therefore, there is now no condemnation for those who are in Christ Jesus." God delivered grace to me as an atonement for all my sins. I wrote the following poem as an attempt to get my head around this.

Only One with a Blemish

I woke up in the narrow light of dawn,
Thinking about life
Here and after
With all its joy,
With pain and strife.

I thought this is a great day.
I could fall in love today.
It could be dark, and I could go mad,
Or it could be my last here.

My father was healthy and robust.
He died quickly from the cancer and was gone.
My mom, tough as iron,
Suffered bouts of mania, finally
Lost her mind, and went home.

Our twins died in the womb.
The cord choked out the life.

My last here will be a great day, too, for
Dad will greet me and hug my neck.
No cancer. "I've been cleared since seventy-eight."
Mom will caress my hair,
And we'll chat with sanity and depth.

My little girls will be dazzling,
At home in their heaven.

In heaven, all the stars of creation will be singing,
No pain.
No cancer.
No madness.
No war.
No blemish, all perfect and restored.

Except for One.
"But, where is Jesus? Where is my Lord?"
He's the only One with a blemish or scar,
The sacred wounds,
Wounds that make every day a great day, here and after.

Some birds pecked on the windows of a farmer's house in the middle of winter. They saw the light and were trying to get in from the cold. The farmer walked to his barn, turned the lights on and tried to wave the birds away from his house into the protected space of the barn. The birds just kept pecking away at the window. The farmer thought, *If only I could be a bird, I could communicate with those birds and lead them safely into the barn.*

That's what God did for us. In Old Testament days, God communicated with mankind. Some people ignored or failed to adhere to His Word. So God became a human so He could communicate directly with us.

God sent Jesus to communicate directly with people. Prior to Jesus, people sacrificed animals to atone for sins. Jesus is fully God and was fully human. Jesus only discipled twelve ordinary men, but God's message of love and grace has traveled around the world. Think of what we could achieve if we'd simply focus deeply the message of Jesus.

The Case for Christ

I was glad to have Ron Johnston and John Drueke walking with me today. Walking with these two guys is like walking with two of the Lord's disciples. Ron has a divinity degree, and I call him Barnabas because he always carries a big smile and distributes compliments and encouragement wherever he goes. John is one of the most well-read laymen I know. He's like Old Faithful—he is always there with that giant, gentle smile, showing his love for the Lord.

In our men's prayer group, we studied *The Case for Christ* by Lee Strobel. As we walked, Ron, John, and I had a terrific conversation about Strobel's book and the divinity and humanity of Jesus.

Strobel, a lawyer and investigative reporter, was an atheist who set out to investigate his wife's newfound belief after she accepted Jesus as her personal Savior. He interviewed many experts along three lines of investigation: 1. the record from eyewitnesses inside and outside the Bible; 2. Jesus Himself; 3. the resurrection, the medical evidence of sweating drops of blood, and Jesus's appearances after His rising from the dead.

The results from his investigation proved to Strobel that the evidence is overwhelming. Jesus was who he claimed to be—the Son of God.

There is more physical evidence and more eyewitness accounts of Jesus's ministry on the earth than any other event in history. There have been more books written about the life and ministry of Jesus Christ than anyone else. Jesus's virgin birth, his violent death on a cross, and His resurrection as the atonement for the sins of mankind are evidences of God's divine, never-ending love for mankind. God allowed His Son to be sacrificed for my sins and for your sins, the greatest possible gift we could receive.

Paying the Cost

Once when leaving the Chicago O'Hare airport and traveling on one of the toll roads around the city, I waved a man on to move ahead of me in the toll line. Within a few minutes, he had moved through the toll booth, and it was my turn. As I moved into the booth with my quarter in my hand, the booth agent said, "He paid your toll; you can move on through." I wish I'd had the presence of mind to say, "Please pay for the guy behind me with this quarter." But stunned, I moved on through the line and merged into the traffic flow.

During my visit to Chicago, I told everyone about the quarter the man had spent paying my toll and what wonderful people there must be in all of Chicago. Whenever I traveled the tollway again, I gave the booth agent an extra quarter for the person behind me. As I've returned to Chicago from time to time, I've continued this practice although the cost of the tolls has increased. There is great joy in knowing someone will feel as good as I did that week when someone else paid my toll.

If I could get excited over a quarter, how much greater is it to share with others the joy of Jesus's sacrifice for me and for you. He paid the price for our sins and offers to us all the opportunity of eternal life.

There's more good news about what Jesus did for us. Not only did He take the punishment for our sins, He forgets we ever sinned. To tell the truth, I would not want to go to heaven if God remembered all my sins. I can imagine showing up and having God say, "Troy Allen Waugh! Here's a list of what you did wrong. We've been waiting to deal with you!" Thank God that our sins are blotted out when we yield to Christ, buried in the deepest sea, and remembered no more (Acts 3:19, Psalm 51:9).

Good News

Karl Barth, the Swiss-German theologian, delivered a lecture at the University of Chicago Divinity School. The president of the seminary said he would ask Dr. Barth one question on behalf of the audience. He asked, "Of all the theological insights you have ever had, which do you consider to be the greatest of them all?"

The students, professors, and attendees sat with anticipation as Karl Barth thought for a while and finally said, "The greatest theological insight I have ever had is this: Jesus loves me, this I know, for the Bible tells me so!"

Troy Waugh

"Jesus loves me, this I know, for the Bible tells me so" is a simple refrain, but it is deep theologically and has been imbedded into my brain, heart, and soul from the time I was a baby by my parents, my teachers, and my pastors.

―❦―

Sunday afternoon about 5:00 p.m., a group of our family and friends assembled at MM 434 to walk across the Natchez Trace's double-arch bridge together. There are only two of this kind in America—here and in Los Alamos, New Mexico. Breathtakingly beautiful, the bridge sits 155 feet above Highway 96 West and has won thirteen engineering design awards.

We had reached MM 438—only seven miles to go, which we will finish on Monday.

Chapter 31

God and Government

It's a good thing we don't get all the government we pay for.
—Will Rogers

August 4, 2014

JONATHAN AND I BEGAN OUR day at MM 438 at 6:00 a.m. and walked until 7:30, covering four miles at a very good pace. His cheery and positive attitude about life pepped me up. I was looking forward to our friends joining us this afternoon to complete the walk.

Today's Reflections

While I had some quiet time early this morning, I was able to really listen to the Holy Spirit. I began to think on a subject that has been on my heart for a long time: God and government. I sensed the Lord encouraging me to reflect this day on how government and God relate to each other.

Jesus never challenged the form of the secular government, nor did He make any suggestions how it should be established. His concerns were much higher.

Yet people from all segments of the political spectrum can offer up scriptural references as to how God supports their party or their beliefs. Some people advocate that God calls for socialism, while others believe He recommends a limited secular government. Still others would have you believe God promotes a government that administers vast social health and welfare programs. Many people hear the Lord's calling to be hospitable to the alien as a call for open borders.

Jesus was law-abiding, as were his earthly parents. Joseph and Mary traveled ninety miles to abide with the decree for a census. Jesus respected the secular government, and He was careful to not violate the Law. Near the time of Jesus's crucifixion, the local governor Pilate said, "I find no basis for a charge against this man."

Jesus told the spies whom the teachers of the Law had sent to entrap him with their questions about paying taxes, "Then give back to Caesar what is Caesar's, and to God what is God's" (Luke 20:25). Jesus recognized secular governments existed to maintain order. They required citizens to be honest, pay taxes, and uphold the law.

The Law of Love

Jesus did give us some guidance in the two most important commandments. He said we are to love God with all our heart, soul, and mind, and our neighbor as ourselves. If all the Law hangs on these two commandments, then loving God is miles above loving a secular government.

One manner of loving God is to advocate for secular laws and to elect leaders who are in alignment with loving God and loving our neighbor. Sadly, many politicians use deceit and very unloving methods to gain office while pandering to the Christian vote. Many times it is difficult to tell the sincere politicians from the charlatans.

I feel Christians have a responsibility to know what moral and legal policies align with loving God and loving our neighbor. I support Christian leaders who are willing to provide guidance in these positions. Pastors guide us in raising our children, using our money, living in our communities, functioning in the business world, and various other aspects of life. Why should they not provide insight into laws that please God?

There are many issues regarding loving God and our neighbor that are not clear cut. Issues like poverty, war, taxes, the budget, foreign aid, immigration, abortion, the death penalty, the environment, same-sex marriage, pornography, poverty, and education are often thorny. You may find Christians on both sides of an argument.

As Christians, we should pray for the Lord's discernment regarding our stand on issues. We need special discernment on whether a politician is pandering to us or is serious about solving problems. The United States has great need for moral guidance. I am convinced Christians should study, speak publicly about, and advocate for laws that line up with loving God and loving our neighbor.

God as King

In the Old Testament, God used Moses to lead the Israelites out of slavery. He gave them a set of laws that formed the basis for a new government, the purpose of which was to bring order to their society. That government was a monarchy with God as king. This was a government of the heart and of basic morality. In other words, religion ran the government, and laws were based on loyalty to the one true God.

With God as their king, Israel had no central secular government. As long as the people served God, He protected, led, and fed them. Israelites were led by local elders, priests, prophets, and judges. When the people strayed from God through idol worship, sexual immorality, and violence, God removed His protection. When the people strayed from the Lord, they were constantly vulnerable to war and slavery by other nations, and all suffered dreadfully.

After years of decentralized local leadership, the Israelites demanded a king. The prophet Samuel warned them of the consequences (1 Sam. 8:11–18). A king with centralized power would result in a military-industrial complex, a draft, loss of freedoms, heavy taxation, and confiscation.

Democracy Developed

Neither in the Old nor New Testaments can we find where people voted for their leaders or where leaders served for a specified term of office. In Athens, Greece, a new form of government called democracy was created. In democracy, people elected leaders who served limited terms. The system was not ideal as not everyone had a vote.

Jesus did not advocate democracy. He didn't ask his disciples, Can we get a consensus on going to the temple? or Let's vote on who will be on my executive team. While democracy has evolved as an excellent form of secular government, the Bible doesn't advocate it. Of course, neither does the Bible mention socialism or libertarianism.

Throughout the ages, democracy has not proven perfect. Articulate politicians buy votes with the people's own money. Winston Churchill said democracy is the worst form of government—except for all the other forms that have been tried.

Human nature is such that people do not have incentive to work very hard unless they keep a substantial portion of their income for that work. Someone quipped, "It's becoming very difficult to support the government in the manner in which it has become accustomed."

A pure democracy has one major drawback: there are no individual freedoms for the minority. In a pure democracy, the forty-nine percent are governed by the majority.

Our founders installed a modified form of government—a democratic republic. In this form, they designed three coequal branches of a weak federal government. States were to make their own laws, as long as they conformed to the US Constitution.

Christians in Government

I do believe Christians must influence our government according to God's moral standards while insisting on protecting the freedom of religion. There is both Old and New Testament support for Christians influencing governments.

Daniel spoke to King Nebuchadnezzar. Joseph influenced Pharaoh. Moses demanded freedom for the people of Israel. John the Baptist preached the gospel of Jesus and advised leaders about the moral right and wrong of their policies. Paul spoke of faith in Jesus Christ, righteousness, and self-control before the Roman governor Felix.

America was founded in great part on individual and religious freedom. Early pioneers did not want a government-mandated religion. It is clear that God's guidance was involved in the founding and government formation of the United States. With God's guidance and a democratic republic form of secular government, we have become the most powerful nation in the history of the world.

Our Present Polarization

America is increasingly polarized. I am worried we are presently engaging in a cold civil war in our country. The trajectory is similar to that of 1860, when the US was divided and headed for a hot civil war.

Geographically, people in states such as California and New York have radically different worldviews than people in the central part of the country. There has been discussion of secession of states, as in the 1860s. In 1860, Mississippi and South Carolina were the two wealthiest states in the nation as California and New York are today. Secession led to the Civil War.

Today, about half the people in the country desire normal politics where we all agree on common goals and we debate the methods to achieve those goals. Another large group promotes regime politics, which pits one group against the other for the sake of power.

Many Americans want to abide by our Constitution as it was written, amended, and modified. Others want a living Constitution, first envisioned by Woodrow Wilson, which adapts to popular fads and is changed by unelected judges and bureaucrats.

One large group believes our freedom and rights are derived from natural laws in that we are all human, created by God, without regard to ethnicity, gender, or class. Others believe rights should be based upon membership in certain groups, and they pit one against the other.

One group still believes government exists to serve people and officials should be elected by the people. Others believe our rules should be made by unelected officials who know better how to run our lives than we do.

One large group believes in the sanctity of life, especially the unborn. Others are adamant that the rights of a woman to terminate the life of her baby supersede the rights of her living unborn child. One group believes in free speech. Another group believes in limiting speech to the current politically correct fad.

One group believes in freedom of religion, the other freedom from religion. Groups led by the American Civil Liberties Union (ACLU) attempt to force us to exclude religion from the public square. The ACLU has succeeded in removing prayer from schools and before sporting events. They attempt to limit any discussion of God. The ACLU twists the ideal of freedom of religion to mean freedom *from* all religious influence.

Advocating for Moral Laws

Governments make an enormous difference in our lives. While we can vote for or against political issues, not many are also spiritual issues. For example, I advocate lower taxes, but the Bible does not endorse low taxes. All it says is we are to pay taxes honestly. Other issues like immigration, health care, and the environment are not clear spiritual issues addressed in the Bible, but they may have religious overtones.

Conservative Christians, of which I am one, argue that big government decreases our freedom by instituting more rules by unelected administrators. My liberal, progressive friends want government to provide a vast array of social, health, and welfare services.

The Bible teaches a leader in the church should be a godly, moral, ethical person no matter who is in political office. The Bible commands us to respect and honor them whether we voted for them or not, whether they are of the political party we prefer or not.

In our Declaration of Independence, the first two sentences mention God twice:

> When in the Course of human events, it becomes necessary for one people to dissolve the political bands which have connected them with another, and to assume among the Powers of the earth, the separate and equal station to which the Laws of Nature and of Nature's God entitle them, a decent respect to the opinions of mankind requires that they should declare the causes which impel them to the separation.
>
> We hold these truths to be self-evident, that all men are created equal, that they are endowed by their Creator with certain unalienable Rights . . .

The signers said the purpose of government is to protect the rights given to people by God ("endowed by their Creator"). This is hardly "excluding religion" from government.

If pastors and other church leaders teach people how to raise their children, have good marriages, love their neighbors as themselves, why can they not teach about good government?

At 5:00 p.m. on Monday, August 4, 2015, twenty of our friends met us at a rest stop near MM 441, and we walked the final three miles to the end of the trace and a celebration at the Loveless Café.

Praise the holy God in heaven, He gave me an amazing gift!

I was so very thankful for the friends who joined us to celebrate that night.

Afterward, I felt so exhausted and regretted I didn't have some God-breathed words of thanks for all the folks who had supported me during these arduous three months. Many people gave money to CCF, others called me, sent emails of encouragement, or came to celebrate the completion of my walk.

I believe my walk on the Natchez Trail during the summer of 2014 was God's method of shaking me loose from the regrets of my past and firming up my spiritual belief system so I could walk into the future closer to Jesus.

Afterword

Reflections on the Journey

I PRAY THAT SOME OF the thoughts and experiences in this book have been thought-provoking and feeling-provoking as well—feelings inspired by the majesty of the Lord and the wonder of our human experience of walking with Jesus.

During my walk, I experienced a renewal in my spiritual, physical, mental, and emotional journey. As I have shared with you some things I learned, my hope is you will be inspired to deepen your own walk with Jesus and open yourself to His power and thereby experience Him in new ways.

I don't have a special relationship with God—our relationship is one every person can have. My prayer is that you will develop a deeper relationship with God by listening to His voice through His urgings or His audible direction. I hope my story can inspire you to pray more, and as you pray, that you will allow God to speak back. God speaks to each one of us in unique ways that apply only to us.

During this last month, God showed me His supernatural powers in a variety of ways. He has spoken to me audibly, through His Holy Spirit, and given me encouragement. He modified the weather for my safety and sent me an angel to encourage me. I have learned to walk with Him daily and lead my life to honor Him.

My particular walk was primarily about me being obedient to God's direction. I walked also to raise awareness and funds for Community Care Fellowship, a homeless ministry in Nashville started by my friend Ken Powers.

While many people contributed to CCF and thousands of dollars were raised, I will always remember the five crumpled one dollar bills given by J.D., who emptied his pockets for our cause at the end of a long hot day.

Acknowledgments

GOD PROVIDED SEVERAL ANGELS ALONG my journey.

My wife, Sheryl, bore up under my irritability while I was training. Then she spent the entire thirty-five days of my walk supporting me, driving me, feeding me, rubbing my tired legs, medicating my wounded feet, and loving me. While she was initially skeptical about the walk, she accepted God's direction and became my daily and hourly Number One Encourager. She dropped me off and picked me up, first in the mornings, then in the evenings, for my two walking sessions each day. Some days she walked with me. Most days, she journaled, deepened her own walk with God, and wrote some of the most beautiful notes and emails to our friends.

My stepdaughter Leanna was extremely helpful as my physical coach. Leanna is a triathlete, coach, and teacher. When she heard about my intention to walk the trace, she gave me ideas on training, hydration, and diet. She was excited with me and gave me lots of encouragement.

Minister Russ Corley, CEO of Encouragement Ministries and minister of Madison Church of Christ, was a daily prayer warrior and encourager for me. Russ prayed for me several times a day, sent me encouraging texts, and called me at least once a day. At Encouragement Ministries, Russ's normal routine is to counsel the sick and broken. I believe God paired Russ with me so He could speak through Russ to encourage me to live out God's purpose in my life. Russ and his wife, Jackie, even met up with us in Alabama to walk with me on a portion of the trace.

My brothers from the Praying Men of Leiper's Fork (the men's prayer group at Hillsboro United Methodist Church in Leiper's Fork, Tennessee) prayed for me, called me, sent me texts, and encouraged me. Lenny Grasso, Carl Gallauresi, Ron Johnston, Keith Elder, David Cooper, Jonathan Hughes, Randy Odom, Kris Gernentz, Kevin Dakin, and others walked with me a few miles in the last few days of my walk.

Other wonderful angels were Buster and Darlene Wolfe, our dear friends and leaders of our monthly Bible study group. Buster called me, prayed for me, and texted me regularly. Darlene talked with Sheryl daily, and Buster and Darlene came to Alabama as well to walk with Sheryl and me. Walking across the Tennessee River on the Natchez Trace Bridge was one of the most exhilarating days of the journey.

One of my most special angels was Jonathan Hughes. Jonathan is one of my closest friends at Hillsboro United Methodist Church. Chairman of our ushers, he works for the Williamson County School System and runs his farm in Leiper's Fork. Jonathan texted me, called me, and walked with me forty-eight miles of the journey. As we talked, we became better friends along the way.

Rev. Pat Freudenthal, then executive director of Community Care Fellowship, encouraged me, sent me notes, and despite her recent ankle surgery, walked the last few miles with me. Reverend Pat has been one of the most faithful and productive executive directors of Community Care Fellowship since its founding in 1984 by my friend Ken Powers.

A wonderful group walked with me across the Natchez Trace Bridge on Sunday evening on August 3: Sheryl Waugh; Kevin Dakin; Lenny, Lori and Millie Grasso; Dustin Gatlin; Jonathan and Betty Hughes; Gladys Johnson; Kris and Lisa Gernentz; Cherry Lane Darken; Jeff and Sonja Fulmer; Leanna, Jason and Daniel Hunt; and Brian Waugh. Other friends drove by and waved.

Joining us for the last leg were Sheryl Waugh, Ann Whitecotton, Alice Waugh, David Mason, Buster and Darlene Wolfe, Pastor Betty Proctor-Bjorgo, Judy Peden, Leanna McCaleb, Jason and Daniel Hunt, and Pat Freudenthal.

Waiting for us at the Loveless Café were other friends with banners

Acknowledgments

and flowers to celebrate the completion of the walk: Floyd and Dorothy Raines, John and Fern Fisher, Martha Greene, Jay and Sally Rogers, Robin Gilliam, Kim McCaleb, Margaret Wilburn, Russ and Jackie Corley, Deborah MacDonald, Don and Gretchen McCance, Cherry Lane Darken, and Rick Dunlap.

Order Information

REDEMPTION P
PRESS

To order additional copies of this book, please visit:
www.redemption-press.com

Or call toll free 1-844-2REDEEM

CPSIA information can be obtained
at www.ICGtesting.com
Printed in the USA
FSHW020645180620
71298FS